CONFERENCING HANDBOOK

The New
<u>REAL</u> JUSTICE®
Training Manual

CONFERENCING HANDBOOK

The New
REAL JUSTICE
Training Manual

by
Terry O'Connell
Ben Wachtel
Ted Wachtel

The Piper's Press
Pipersville, Pennsylvania

10 9 8 7 6 5 4 3 2 1
First Edition

The Piper's Press
P.O. Box 400
Pipersville, PA 18947

Terry O'Connell, Ben Wachtel and Ted Wachtel
Conferencing Handbook:
The New Real Justice® Training Manual

Library of Congress Catalog Number: 99-70193

ISBN 0-9633887-5-4

About This Manual

This manual is a procedural guide to facilitating Real Justice conferences. It focuses on lesser incidents of wrongdoing, the vast majority of offenses. This manual will not, by itself, prepare readers to facilitate a conference for serious offenses involving severe trauma for victims.

Real Justice provides training using this manual as a resource. However, the manual is available to anyone, and its use in a training does not signify that Real Justice is affiliated with that training.

Acknowledgments

The authors thank the following people and conferencing programs for allowing samples of their program literature and forms to be used in this handbook:

- Gena Gerard and the Central City Community Partnership, Minneapolis, Minnesota
- Kay Whelan and Hawke's Bay Restorative Justice Te Puna Wai Ora, Inc., Hastings, New Zealand
- David Hines and the Woodbury Police Department, Woodbury, Minnesota
- Lawrie Parker, Vickie Shoap and the Piedmont Dispute Resolution Center, Warrenton, Virginia
- Glenn Kummery, Bruce Taylor and Central Bucks School District, Doylestown, Pennsylvania

Contents

Figures

Documents

Chapter 1:
The Script

A conference is a forum where people deal with wrongdoing and conflict. All participants can speak, express their feelings and, most importantly, have a say in the outcome. A conference is a democratic experience in which those most affected by a problem decide how to respond to it.

The conference facilitator brings the participants together, creates a safe and supportive environment, keeps the process focused and records the decisions of the group. The conference facilitator does *not* make or influence the decisions, but lets participants express themselves and find their own creative solutions. The best conference facilitators guide the process, yet remain in the background. They encourage, but do not control or dictate.

The script is the heart of the conference. It is a simple, reliable tool which allows a facilitator to run a conference successfully without extensive mediation or counseling training. First the script prescribes a series of open-ended questions which encourage people to respond "affectively," that is, to express how they were affected by the issue that brought them together. Next the script provides participants an opportunity to exchange ideas, develop a plan to address the conflict or wrongdoing, and repair the harm that resulted. Finally the script invites participants to an informal, post-conference social gathering, when refreshments are served and participants mingle and talk.

Please read the conference script on the next three pages now. (Facilitators should photocopy this script for their use in running conferences.)

The script is the heart of the conference. It is a simple, reliable tool which allows a facilitator to run a conference successfully without extensive mediation or counseling training.

Conference Facilitator's Script

1. Preamble

"Welcome. As you know, my name is (your name) **and I will be facilitating this conference."**

Now introduce each conference participant and state his/her relationship to the offender/s or victim/s.

"Thank you all for attending. I know that this is difficult for all of you, but your presence will help us deal with the matter that has brought us together. This is an opportunity for all of you to be involved in repairing the harm that has been done."

"This conference will focus on an incident which happened (state the date, place and nature of offense without elaborating). **It is important to understand that we will focus on what** (offender name/s) **did and how that unacceptable behavior has affected others. We are not here to decide whether** (offender name/s) **is**/are **good or bad. We want to explore in what way people have been affected and hopefully work toward repairing the harm that has resulted. Does everyone understand this?"**

"(Offender name/s) has/have **admitted his**/her/their **part in the incident."**

Say to offender/s: **"I must tell you that you do not have to participate in this conference and are free to leave at any time, as is anyone else. If you do leave, the matter may be referred to court**/handled by the school disciplinary policy/ handled in another way.**"**

"This matter, however, may be finalized if you participate in a positive manner and comply with the conference agreement."

Say to offender/s: **"Do you understand?"**

2. Offender/s

"We'll start with (one of offenders' names).**"**

If there is more than one offender, have each respond to all of the following questions.

- **"What happened?"**
- **"What were you thinking about at the time?"**
- **"What have you thought about since the incident?"**
- **"Who do you think has been affected by your actions?"**
- **"How have they been affected?"**

3. Victim/s

If there is more than one victim, have each respond to all of the following questions.

- **"What was your reaction at the time of the incident?"**
- **"How do you feel about what happened?"**
- **"What has been the hardest thing for you?"**
- **"How did your family and friends react when they heard about the incident?"**

4. Victim Supporters

Have each respond to all of the following questions.

- **"What did you think when you heard about the incident?"**
- **"How do you feel about what happened?"**
- **"What has been the hardest thing for you?"**
- **"What do you think are the main issues?"**

5. Offender Supporters

To parent/caregiver ask: **"This has been difficult for you, hasn't it? Would you like to tell us about it?"**

Have each respond to all of the following questions.

- **"What did you think when you heard about the incident?"**
- **"How do you feel about what happened?"**
- **"What has been the hardest thing for you?"**
- **"What do you think are the main issues?"**

6. Offender/s

Ask the offender/s: **"Is there anything you want to say at this time?"**

7. Reaching an Agreement

Ask the victim/s: **"What would you like from today's conference?"**

Ask the offender/s to respond.

At this point, the participants discuss what should be in the final agreement. Solicit comments from participants.

It is important that you ask the offender/s to respond to each suggestion before the group moves to the next suggestion, asking **"What do you think about that?"** Then determine that the offender/s agree/s before moving on. Allow for negotiation.

As the agreement develops, clarify each item and make the written document as specific as possible, including details, deadlines and follow-up arrangements.

As you sense that the agreement discussion is drawing to a close, say to the participants: **"Before I prepare the written agreement, I'd like to make sure that I have accurately recorded what has been decided."**

Read the items in the agreement aloud and look to the participants for acknowledgment. Make any necessary corrections.

8. Closing the Conference

"Before I formally close this conference, I would like to provide everyone with a final opportunity to speak. Is there anything anyone wants to say?"

Allow for participants to respond and when they are done, say: **"Thank you for your contributions in dealing with this difficult matter. Congratulations on the way you have worked through the issues. Please help yourselves to some refreshments while I prepare the agreement."**

Allow participants ample time to have refreshments and interact. The informal period after the formal conference is very important.

Origins of the Script

The script for conferencing originated with one of the authors of this manual, Terry O'Connell, a community policing sergeant in Wagga Wagga, New South Wales, Australia, in 1991.

Conferencing began two years earlier in New Zealand as part of the Children, Youth and Families Act of 1989. That legislation stemmed from discontent among the Maori, the indigenous people of New Zealand, with the way courts dealt with their young people in criminal and social welfare matters. After convening a commission to study the problem, the government decided that a wide range of juvenile justice offenses and child welfare cases would be dealt with through a process called a "family group conference." Instead of going to court, the government would bring together the extended family of a child or youth to develop a plan to address the problem. Although the new process applied to all New Zealand children and youth, it reflected the Maori tradition that the individual's family and community should be directly involved in any response to wrongdoing and conflict, a practice typical of most aboriginal or indigenous people.

New Zealand's bold experiment in empowering families to take greater responsibility for their own children has influenced philosophy and practice among social workers and criminal justice professionals throughout the world. Among those influenced was Terry O'Connell, who was working with a local committee of citizens in Wagga Wagga to develop new responses to juvenile crime. After exploring the idea, the citizen group decided to implement conferencing in their community.

Never having seen an actual conference, O'Connell improvised. He borrowed the concept and kept the name "family group conference," but changed the procedure substantially when he adapted it as a community policing response to juvenile offenses. Having a police officer facilitate the conference, rather than a social worker, was distinctly different from the New Zealand approach. O'Connell also wrote a script for the facilitator to follow, which simplified conducting conferences and helped ensure a reliable result.

The Wagga Wagga model of conferencing also gave the victim's family and friends a chance to be involved,

New Zealand's bold experiment in empowering families to take greater responsibility for their own children has influenced philosophy and practice among social workers and criminal justice professionals throughout the world.

The Wagga Wagga conference model was a carefully orchestrated emotional encounter between young offenders, their victims and their respective friends and families that typically resulted in a written plan to repair the harm caused by the offense.

unlike the original New Zealand process. New Zealand has since changed its law to provide victim supporters a role in family group conference criminal cases. Another significant difference was that the New Zealand legislation prescribes an opportunity for the family of the child to "caucus," that is, to meet separately with only family members present, excluding social workers, police and others from being in the room. The government representatives can subsequently overrule the decision of the family, but only if the plan is deemed "impracticable or inconsistent with the principles" of the legislation. The caucus is not part of the scripted conference process developed by O'Connell.

The Wagga Wagga conference model was a carefully orchestrated emotional encounter between young offenders, their victims and their respective friends and families that typically resulted in a written plan to repair the harm caused by the offense. When victims and other conference participants began singing the praises of conferencing, the practice spread. The Australian media started reporting about family group conferences. Australian educators began using the process with incidents of school misconduct in 1994. Young offenders, if they agreed to participate, were diverted from the normal court or school disciplinary procedures.

In 1994 a Winston Churchill Fellowship enabled O'Connell to travel and tell others about his work with family group conferencing, which had come to be called by various names, including "community accountability conferencing," "diversionary conferencing" or simply "conferencing." His trip fostered the adoption of conferencing by police and others in the United States, Canada and the United Kingdom.

During this trip, Ted Wachtel, a co-author of this manual, heard O'Connell speak at a Bucks County Juvenile Court luncheon in Doylestown, Pennsylvania. Wachtel is the executive director of the Community Service Foundation, a non-profit agency providing counseling, education and residential services to troubled and delinquent youth in southeastern Pennsylvania. After hearing O'Connell speak, Wachtel decided to found Real Justice, an international non-profit program dedicated to fostering the use of the scripted model of conferencing and related restorative practices throughout the world.

Variations on the Script

When Real Justice began in 1994, conferencing addressed only juvenile offenses and school discipline issues. Conferencing is now used for a wide range of offenses in communities, schools, college campuses, institutions and workplaces. The script presented in this chapter is specifically for conferences dealing with criminal offenses and incidents of wrongdoing where offenders have admitted responsibility for the act and there is an identifiable victim.

Conferencing can also be used for truancy, drug possession and other "victimless" offenses, probation and parole violations, and interpersonal conflicts. It can sometimes be used when responsibility for an offense is not clear, but the parties affected are willing to participate in a conference. This handbook focuses on conferencing for incidents involving distinct victims and offenders, but the conference script and preparation can be modified to address other types of offenses, conflicts and situations. Sometimes family and friends of offenders are embarrassed and concerned by the offender's actions and therefore indirectly victimized. Literature from the Piedmont Dispute Resolution Center conferencing program in Warrenton, Virginia, on pages 141-145, suggests how the conference process and script can be adopted to address school truancy or victimless offenses.

Conferencing can also be used for truancy, drug possession and other "victimless" offenses, probation and parole violations, and interpersonal conflicts.

Silvan Tomkins's Affect Theory

Silvan Tomkins's psychological theory of human affect, as articulated by Donald Nathanson (1992), helps explain why the scripted conference is so effective.

Conferencing encourages free expression of affect, the biological basis for emotion and feeling. The conference allows expression of true feelings, while minimizing negative affect and maximizing positive affect. In Tomkins's theory, this kind of environment is the ideal setting for healthy human relationships.

The conference script uses open-ended questions that encourage the display of all nine basic affects (see Figure 1 on page 24) which Tomkins identified as existing in every human being. Tomkins presented most affects as hyphenated word pairs which name the least and most intensive expressions of that affect. When a conference begins, people are feeling *disgust*, *dissmell*

Figure 1

The Nine Affects

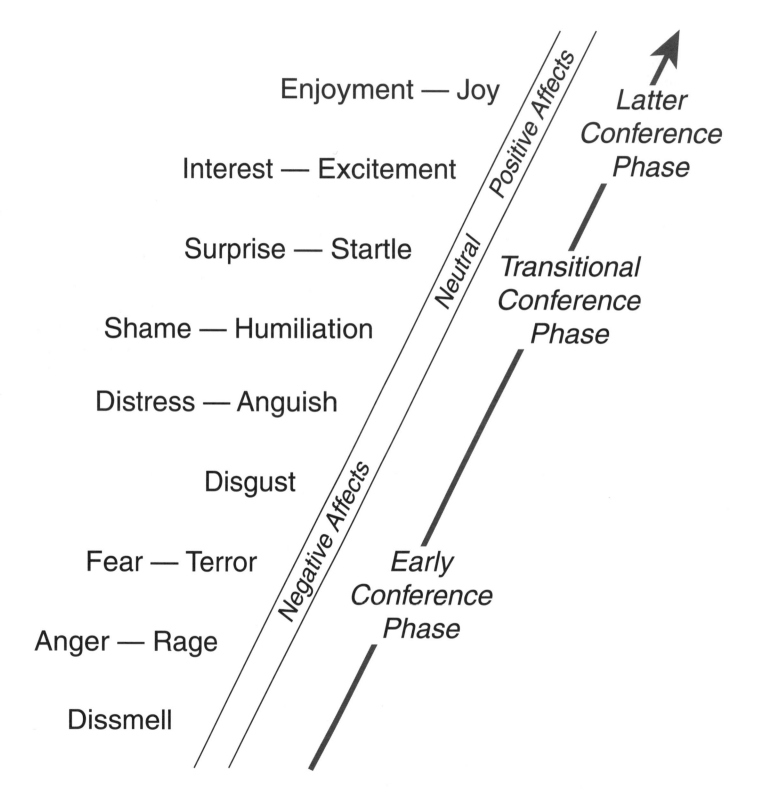

Enjoyment — Joy

Interest — Excitement

Surprise — Startle

Shame — Humiliation

Distress — Anguish

Disgust

Fear — Terror

Anger — Rage

Dissmell

Positive Affects

Neutral

Negative Affects

Latter Conference Phase

Transitional Conference Phase

Early Conference Phase

Adapted from Nathanson, 1992

(which originated biologically as a response to offensive odor), *anger-rage*, *distress-anguish*, *fear-terror* and *shame-humiliation*. These six negative affects are the most prevalent when participants first enter the conference room and sit nervously as the conference begins.

When participants respond to the scripted questions, they may express any or all of those negative affects or feelings. Anger, distress, fear and shame are diminished through sharing. Their expression helps to reduce their intensity.

As the conference proceeds people experience a transition characterized by the neutral affect of *surprise-startle*. Victims, offenders and their supporters are usually surprised by what people say in the conference and how much better they begin to feel. When the conference reaches the agreement phase, participants are usually expressing the positive affects of *interest-excitement* and *enjoyment-joy*.

People recognize the affects seen on others' faces and tend to respond with the same affect. When one is angry, others become angry. When one feels better and smiles, so do others. Tomkins called this "affective resonance" or empathy. Through affective resonance, conference participants make the emotional journey together, feeling each other's feelings as they travel from anger and distress and shame to interest and enjoyment.

The prospective conference facilitator can take comfort in knowing that Tomkins's affect theory is reliably demonstrated by the scripted conference process. People consistently move from negative to positive feelings in the safe and structured environment created by the script.

Conference participants make the emotional journey together, feeling each other's feelings as they travel from anger and distress and shame to interest and enjoyment.

Reintegrative Shaming

Tomkins teaches us that shame is a basic affect occurring spontaneously in all human beings when confronted about their wrongdoing. John Braithwaite, in *Crime, Shame and Reintegration* (1989) advises that the experience of dealing with shame should be reintegrative, not stigmatizing.

Braithwaite's sociological theory of "reintegrative shaming" suggests that Western society's current strategies for responding to crime and wrongdoing may actually be doing more harm than good. Schools and courts

Reintegration involves separating the deed from the doer so that society clearly disapproves of the crime or inappropriate behavior, but acknowledges the intrinsic worth of the individual.

punish and humiliate offenders without offering a way to make amends, right the wrong or shed their "offender" label. Instead, offenders are stigmatized, alienated and pushed into society's growing negative subcultures. They join the others in their school or community who feel excluded from the mainstream and become a source of persistent trouble.

Braithwaite says societies that reintegrate offenders back into the community have a lower crime rate than those that stigmatize and alienate wrongdoers. Reintegration involves *separating the deed from the doer* so that society clearly disapproves of the crime or inappropriate behavior, but acknowledges the intrinsic worth of the individual. The conference script emphasizes that distinction by stating that, "It is important to understand that we will focus on what (offender name/s) did and how that unacceptable behavior has affected others. We are not here to decide whether (offender name/s) is/are good or bad."

In several ways, the conference script helps offenders move beyond their shame toward reintegration. The script provides an opportunity for offenders to take responsibility for their behavior and to apologize. In the agreement phase of the conference, offenders can define specific steps to repair the harm and show good faith, such as making restitution and doing community service. Finally the informal social interaction after the intense conference proceedings brings participants a sense of relief and allows them to interact one-to-one. Victims and offenders and their respective supporters often make gestures of reconciliation during this period, talking, sharing refreshments, shaking hands and sometimes even embracing.

Nathanson's Compass of Shame

Donald Nathanson's "compass of shame" clarifies how people react to and express their shame. (See Figure 2 on page 27.) They usually react with one or more of four general patterns or "scripts" which Nathanson depicts as directions on a compass: *attack other, attack self, withdrawal* and *avoidance*.

When parents or their offending children blame and criticize the school or the police officer when confronted with an offense, they illustrate the *attack other* response.

Figure 2

The Compass of Shame

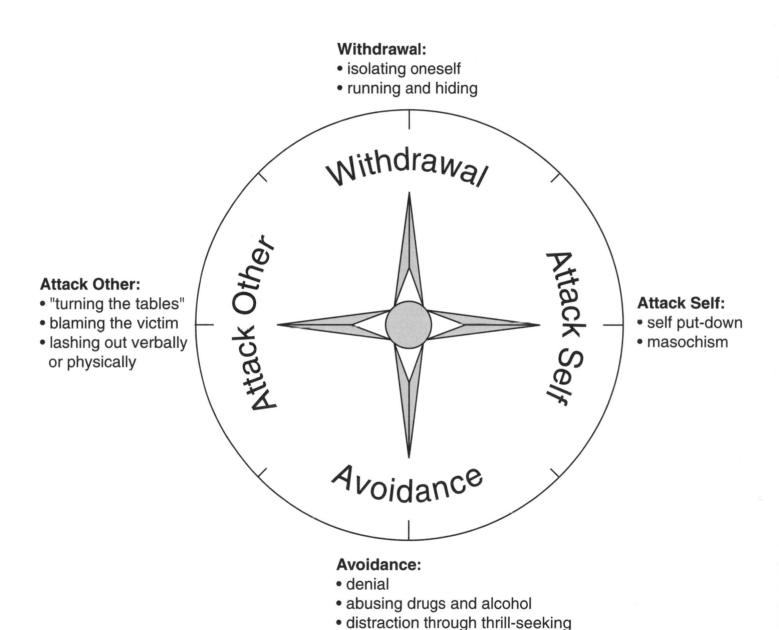

Withdrawal:
• isolating oneself
• running and hiding

Attack Other:
• "turning the tables"
• blaming the victim
• lashing out verbally
  or physically

Attack Self:
• self put-down
• masochism

Avoidance:
• denial
• abusing drugs and alcohol
• distraction through thrill-seeking

Adapted from Nathanson, 1992

These parents or offenders try to avoid shame by putting the responsibility on others. This is the most common response to shame exhibited in today's culture. Another contemporary response is *avoidance*, through alcohol, drug abuse or thrill-seeking behavior, like joy-riding in a stolen car.

Several decades ago, the commonplace responses to shame were *attack self* and *withdrawal*. In *attack self*, the shamed individuals are self-punishing and unreasonably hard on themselves. In *withdrawal*, the shamed individuals hide because they are so overwhelmed by the shame.

These are normal responses to shame. However, they are harmful and need to be addressed. Conferences help people move beyond the compass of shame through acknowledgment and expression of shame and through subsequent reintegration. Because the conference affirms the intrinsic worth of the wrongdoer and condemns only the objectionable behavior, parents and offenders feel less threatened and more readily acknowledge responsibility.

Victims also experience shame. Victims may blame themselves for the offense, withdraw and hide their feelings, and sometimes distract themselves. Victims may lash out at others close to them who are not responsible for the offense. In providing an outlet for expressing feelings and moving beyond shame to resolution and reintegration, the conference is as important to victims as to offenders.

In providing an outlet for expressing feelings and moving beyond shame to resolution and reintegration, the conference is as important to victims as to offenders.

Restorative Justice

Restorative justice is a movement that developed in North America in the 1970s with the advent of victim-offender reconciliation programs. Although conferencing developed independently, it is now considered part of the restorative justice movement. Howard Zehr, in *Changing Lenses: A New Focus for Crime and Justice* (1990), described how restorative justice differs from our current justice system. Borrowing from Zehr, one sees how scripted conferencing differs from our current justice and school disciplinary systems:

1. Our current systems define an offense as a violation of the system, a crime against the state. In a conference an offense is defined as the harm that is done to a person or the community.

2. Our current systems focus on establishing blame or guilt. A conference focuses on solving problems and repairing harm.

3. Our current systems largely ignore the victim. The conference script supports the victims' rights and needs, providing an opportunity for victims to express feelings and help decide the outcome.

4. In our current systems the offender is passive. In a conference the offender is encouraged to take responsibility.

5. Our current systems define accountability as punishment. In a conference accountability means taking responsibility, apologizing and helping to repair the harm.

6. Our current response to crime and wrongdoing focuses on the offender's past behavior. A conference emphasizes the *harmful consequences* of the offender's behavior.

7. Under our current systems the stigma of crime is largely unremovable. The conference helps offenders overcome shame and stigma through appropriate actions.

8. In our current systems there is little encouragement for repentance. In a conference repentance is encouraged and forgiveness is possible.

9. Our current systems depend on professionals for justice. In a conference the facilitator stays in the background. The script encourages the direct involvement of those who have been affected.

10. Our current system is strictly rational. A conference encourages the free expression of emotion.

Why the Script?

The script reflects the human need to express and move beyond negative feelings, repair harm and resolve conflict. The script is easy to follow. It helps the facilitator stay anchored and focused, even in highly emotional situations. It is reliable, based on the experience of thousands of conferences. It is supported by sound psychological and sociological theory. It is a simple model that can be adapted easily to a broad range of offenses, conflicts and situations.

People may be tempted to change the script and make their own version. Some have made changes to the wording and organization of the script, often with undesirable results. Slight variations in wording can cause significant changes in responses.

Our current systems focus on establishing blame or guilt. A conference focuses on solving problems and repairing harm.

Facilitators take an unnecessary risk when they abandon or change the script.

The script presented here is supported by several research studies which have consistently demonstrated high rates of participant satisfaction, perceptions of fairness and offender compliance with conference agreements (McCold & Wachtel, 1998; Moore & Forsythe, 1995; Umbreit & Fercello, 1998, 1999). Rarely has any new process been so thoroughly evaluated.

The argument for sticking to the script can be summarized by the popular maxim, "If it ain't broke, don't fix it." Facilitators take an unnecessary risk when they abandon or change the script.

Chapter 2: When to Run a Conference

Conferences for Offenders and Their Victims

The script in Chapter 1 was written for conferences dealing with criminal offenses and incidents of wrongdoing where offenders have admitted responsibility for the act and there is an identifiable victim. Although conferencing is now used in a variety of situations, including victimless crimes, this chapter focuses on clearcut cases involving victims and offenders.

Conferencing can address victim-offender incidents in many settings—in schools, police departments, probation departments, courts, correctional facilities, workplaces, youth groups, summer camps and on college campuses. Any incident of wrongdoing—where harm has occurred and there is a need to repair that harm—is potentially appropriate for a conference. Within the justice system, the conference may be convened as a police or pre-court diversion, as a means of deciding a sentence or fostering healing after adjudication, or as a reintegration ceremony when an offender is released from an institution to return home. In schools, the conference may serve as an alternative to detention, suspension and expulsion, or as a condition for the offending student returning to school after a suspension.

A single conference should be held for an incident, even when there are multiple offenders or multiple victims. Everyone involved with and affected by that incident should be invited. One offender may agree to participate, one offender may not, and another offender may be unable to attend. Similarly, some victims may participate and others may not. Nevertheless the conference may still be held, regardless of whether everyone attends.

For a conference to proceed, victims and offenders must voluntarily agree to participate, and offenders must

A single conference should be held for an incident, even when there are multiple offenders or multiple victims. Everyone involved with and affected by that incident should be invited.

For a conference to proceed, victims and offenders must voluntarily agree to participate, and offenders must admit to the offense.

admit to the offense. Where victims and offenders differ on facts or degrees of responsibility, facilitators should work to sort them out, making each party aware of the other's view prior to the conference. Victims may still want the conference to proceed, even if offenders have a conflicting perspective or are minimizing their responsibility.

If a conference is held when victims do not want to participate, facilitators should include the victims' perspective, preferably by inviting the victims' family and friends. Victims might write a letter, make an audio or video tape, or convey a message through the facilitator.

Some may question running a conference with offenders or victims who are physically or mentally disabled, mentally ill, emotionally disturbed, very young or very old. While such people may be unable to participate fully in the conference, they and their supporters can still benefit from the experience. Facilitators should enlist supporters who can help these individuals participate in the conference, understand what is happening, and perhaps even interpret their behavior.

When offenders present a less than ideal attitude, facilitators should not avoid conferencing. A conference may help change that attitude. Some facilitators think they can predict which offenders will not participate appropriately or benefit from a conference, but that is unlikely. If facilitators are concerned, they should inform victims how the offenders are acting and let the victims decide if they want to proceed. Many victims simply want a chance to talk directly to offenders. Facilitators should not impose their fears. If no additional harm is likely to occur and victims are prepared for the encounter, a conference is a viable option. The decision to proceed belongs to the victims and offenders.

At the very least, conferences offer a chance for victims to express their feelings directly to offenders. Exchange of affect is usually beneficial. The process of human beings talking to each other will almost always be better than silent avoidance.

Who Should Facilitate the Conference?

A primary factor in deciding to run a conference is whether the facilitator has the experience needed for the particular case. This handbook, even if accompanied by the two-day Real Justice facilitator training, will not prepare someone to facilitate a conference for violent offenses involving severe trauma for victims. However, if the facilitators have sufficient experience in dealing with serious crimes and their victims, they might appropriately facilitate such a conference.

Conferences may be facilitated by professionals as part of their jobs, specialists who are hired as full-time facilitators, screened and trained volunteers, or peers such as schoolmates, fellow inmates or co-workers. Facilitators should not run conferences for incidents that directly affected them or when they have played a counseling or support role with the offenders or victims.

Some people think that police officers or probation officers should not facilitate conferences as part of their professional role. Others believe that only volunteers are neutral enough to facilitate criminal justice conferences. These arbitrary limits on who should facilitate conferences are based on unsupported opinion and stereotyping. Research has consistently contradicted such constraints. A series of studies indicates that conference participants are satisfied with police officers running conferences (McCold & Wachtel, 1998; Moore & Forsythe, 1995, Umbreit & Fercello, 1998).

Conferences often transform the facilitator. Police, probation officers and educators who have become cynical are often surprised by the positive outcomes they see in a conference. Even when offenders later re-offend, the conference provides disheartened professionals with a hopeful glimpse of the potential of offenders and, if nothing else, allows them to see victims gain some healing and closure after a hurtful experience.

Timeframes

In most cases facilitators should move quickly, limiting the time between the incident and the conference to a couple of weeks. Unfortunately paperwork and procedures often interfere, so the timeframe may be longer. If a conference is for a serious offense, victims may need more time to regain their equilibrium and prepare for meeting with the offenders. Grave offenses, like murder, may not result in a conference until years later.

Facilitators should not run conferences for incidents that directly affected them or when they have played a counseling or support role with the offenders or victims.

In most cases facilitators should move quickly, limiting the time elapsed between the incident and the conference to a couple of weeks.

When Not to Run a Conference

Before conferencing, facilitators should learn the details of the incident by speaking with everyone involved, including offenders, victims and their supporters. Certain details may not come to light until the facilitator has begun inviting people and preparing them for the conference. (Conference preparation will be discussed in detail in Chapter 3.)

Political considerations may influence whether to conference. In some jurisdictions, it may be easier and wiser for facilitators to start with lower-level offenses. Lower-level offenses are often simpler to facilitate and the possible negative ramifications are smaller. At first, lesser offenses may be the only cases that are referred anyway. As facilitators gain experience and confidence in their abilities, others will gain confidence in them as well. Then the case flow and levels of offenses are likely to increase.

> *Facilitators should not accept cases that they do not have the experience to handle, such as incidents of severe trauma and sexual, physical or emotional abuse.*

Facilitators should not accept cases that they do not have the experience to handle, such as incidents of severe trauma and sexual, physical or emotional abuse. Conferencing has been successful for these types of cases, but they may require significantly greater preparation, community resources and professional support, as well as relevant experience on the part of the facilitator. This manual is not focused on the most serious offenses, but on the other crime and wrongdoing which comprise the bulk of offenses.

Time or space constraints may prevent facilitators from organizing a full conference. Some incidents may not seem serious enough to run a full conference. However, the level of seriousness is often not easy to discern. The way to find out is to talk to the victims, the ones most affected by the incident.

When a conference is not necessary or feasible, but harm still needs to be repaired, the incident may still be resolved restoratively with an abbreviated conference or by using the questions and philosophy of the script in some other way. Chapter 6 will discuss these informal restorative practices.

Victim Needs

Most professionals attracted to conferencing and restorative justice are offender-focused. They want to help offenders turn their lives in a positive direction. However, when deciding whether to run a conference, they may overlook victim needs. For instance, many of the early police or court conferencing programs were limited to first-time offenders. Thus, if a victim's home was burglarized by a person with a prior offense, that victim was deprived of the opportunity to confront the offender, to have a say in the outcome, and to enjoy the healing and closure that a conference might provide.

Victim needs are the priority in deciding whether to run a conference. According to research in victimology and restorative justice, victims may need:
• an opportunity to express their feelings
• acknowledgment from loved ones about what happened to them
• assurance that what happened was unfair and undeserved
• direct contact with offenders to hear the offender express shame and remorse, answer questions about the offense, and assure them that it won't happen again
• a sense of safety

A conference provides an ideal forum for victims to satisfy these needs.

Victim needs are the priority in deciding whether to run a conference.

Chapter 3: Conference Preparation

Careful preparation is crucial to facilitating successful conferences. Through preparation, facilitators can understand the incident, build rapport with participants, and begin to envision how the conference may unfold. Facilitators should use the Facilitator's Preparation Checklist provided on page 52.

A Note on Language

The terms "victim" and "offender" help facilitators keep track of participants and organize conferences. It would be unwieldy to keep saying "the person who was harmed" or "the person who caused the harm." However, facilitators should never use the terms "victim" and "offender" with conference participants because those terms can be stigmatizing. People should be referred to by their actual names whenever possible.

The terms "incident" and "offense" are used here interchangeably. In reality, for some cases and settings the term "offense" may seem extreme or legalistic. Conversely, for other cases and settings the term "incident" may seem minimizing or euphemistic. Facilitators should judge which term is appropriate.

Choosing a Time and Place

Facilitators should seek a conference room that is readily available or that they can reserve in advance. The room should be large enough for the expected number of participants, be private and free from interruptions, and have access to restrooms. If possible, rooms should also have access to a telephone (that can be turned off during the conference) and a copy machine for duplicating the conference agreement.

The conference location will depend on the jurisdiction but should be convenient, safe and easily accessible. Possibilities include the police station or community policing substation, the courthouse, a public or government building, a community center or school. To preserve the perceived fairness of the process, conferences are rarely held in the homes of conference participants. However, after consulting with the victim, offender and others, facilitators may occasionally deem this appropriate.

Scheduling the conference can sometimes be complicated, especially if there are multiple offenders or victims. Facilitators need a tentative time and date for the conference before contacting possible participants. Facilitators may shuttle between victims and offenders to find a mutually agreeable time. The victims' preference for a meeting time should be given the greatest weight.

Selecting and Inviting Participants

As a courtesy to victims, facilitators should first contact offenders and ensure their willingness to participate in a conference. This will save the victims any disappointment should the offenders decline. If there are multiple offenders, facilitators may begin inviting victims after one offender has agreed.

At a minimum, offenders should admit to the offense to be eligible for a conference, although some offenders may minimize or displace responsibility. Facilitators should address the offenders' need to take full responsibility during a pre-conference meeting.

When contacting people, facilitators explain the conference process and its benefits, answer questions, encourage and secure attendance at the conference, and build rapport and trust. It is *vital* for facilitators to speak with *all* participants before the conference, including victims, offenders, their supporters and others. Conferences where facilitators have not built rapport with all participants are much more likely to be problematic.

Facilitators must tailor their approach to offenders, victims and each set of supporters. Facilitators may create a brochure or information sheet which they can mail or give to people during their pre-conference meetings. The information for victims and their supporters may differ from that provided offenders and their supporters.

It is vital for facilitators to speak with all participants before the conference.

In many cases telephone contact is sufficient to explain the process and build rapport. Often facilitators will prefer to meet with victims and offenders in-person.

Determining who to invite as supporters is an important part of conference preparation.

People sometimes express concern that other participants will be disrespectful or offensive during the conference. In response, facilitators can explain that because participants usually feel conferencing is humane and trust the process, they tend to bring their "best selves" to the circle and participate in a constructive manner.

In many cases telephone contact is sufficient to explain the process and build rapport. Often facilitators will prefer to meet with victims and offenders in-person. This is more time-consuming and not always feasible. However, when the offense is more serious or has complicated dynamics, an in-person meeting may raise participants' trust in the facilitator, improve the quality of the conference, and more fully meet victims' needs. A personal visit may also ensure offenders take full responsibility for the incident, as well as increase the likelihood that victims, offenders and their families will participate. Personal visits are necessary when dealing with more serious offenses, and even with less serious offenses when victims are particularly upset.

When offenders are juveniles, facilitators may be legally required to contact their parents or guardian about the conference and perhaps gain their permission before speaking with the offender. However, if the offenders are of legal age, it may be considered a violation of their privacy to contact their parents without their permission, even if the offender is still in high school or attending a university or college.

Determining who to invite as supporters is an important part of conference preparation. Victims and offenders may nominate anyone they choose. Facilitators may also invite individuals who do not clearly fall into the category of victim, victim supporter or offender supporter, but who have been directly affected by the incident in some way—perhaps someone who witnessed the incident or an investigating police officer. Sometimes victims and offenders make the initial contact with their nominated supporters to tell them about the conference and to let them know the facilitator will call.

Young children may participate in conferences, if they can speak and basically understand what is going on. Even if the conference deals with severe offenses, children can still participate because they have been harmed by those offenses and need healing as much as adults.

Script questions may need to be adapted slightly to a child's level of understanding.

Offenders and victims should not have legal counsel at the conference. The facilitator should advise any attorneys who want to be involved that a conference is not a legal proceeding and that they may attend only as a supporter, like other supporters who are connected to the victim or offender, or as a silent observer sitting outside the circle.

Facilitators should know local laws regarding whether disclosures made in a conference are admissible in court and advise offenders accordingly. In practice, however, the conference almost always settles the matter without further legal proceedings.

When facilitators receive a case, they must learn what will happen if the case does not result in a conference, if no agreement is reached, or if the offender fails to satisfy the agreement. If there is no protocol, facilitators need to discuss the matter with those who have the authority to decide.

It is difficult to say exactly how many people should attend a conference. It depends on the offenders' and victims' support networks, the number of offenders and victims, and the nature of the offense. Most conferences have 8 to 15 participants and run 30 to 90 minutes. Larger conferences may run as long as 2 to 4 hours. Generally the more people in a conference, the longer it will take.

Usually, the more people in a conference, the better, because of the wider variety of personalities. Smaller groups may be dominated by one or two individuals who may or may not be positive influences. In larger groups there is an averaging or normalizing effect, with the more extreme personalities balanced by others in the circle. In fact, facilitators running larger conferences are more likely to find the balance maintained by the participants themselves.

Inviting as many as possible to a conference also offers the opportunity to develop "communities of care" for the victim and offender. Often the victim's community and the offender's community become one community. Because an incident of wrongdoing brings relationships into critical focus, the conference can be a beginning point for establishing and building relationships. The conference allows the building of social

Young children may participate in conferences, if they can speak and basically understand what is going on.

If community representatives are included, they should be coached to speak personally about how the incident made them feel.

bonds which are needed to sustain healthy family and community relationships.

Facilitators with a mediation background often worry about power imbalances, but the conference framework deals with those issues naturally. With supporters for both offenders and victims, the power balance between individuals is evened out. There is no need to have the same number of participants for each "side"—offender and victim. However, if facilitators know that one group is particularly large, they can encourage the other group to bring more supporters.

Inviting official community representatives or others who do not have a direct emotional connection with the incident may be a problem. They sometimes preach or moralize, dampening the affective exchange. If community representatives are included, they should be coached to speak personally about how the incident made them feel.

Contacting Offenders and Young Offenders' Parents

When contacting offenders, facilitators should introduce themselves and explain the purpose of the conference. For example:

"Hi, my name is (facilitator's name). I'm with (facilitator's agency), and I'm working on setting up a conference dealing with (brief description of offense). I'd like to offer you an opportunity to attend a conference instead of (referring the matter to court/handling the matter through school disciplinary procedures/handling the matter in another way). The conference will help us learn how people have been affected by what you did and how to repair the harm that has resulted. We are not going to decide whether you are good or bad. We just want to discuss how your inappropriate behavior affected other people and how to repair the harm."

Facilitators should explain the conference process, who will be present, and what the offender can expect to be asked at the conference. If the offender is not of legal age, facilitators may need to contact the offender's parents or guardian before speaking with the offender.

For offenders and the parents of young offenders, facilitators should describe the advantages of the conference process from their perspective. These include: the opportunity for offenders to understand the consequences of their behavior, learning how the incident has affected their family and friends, helping develop and implement a plan to repair the harm, and disapproving of the offenders' behavior while affirming their worth as members of the community. The conference is an alternative to more punitive disciplinary processes or a way to avoid formal criminal charges. However, conferences are not the "easier" option some might assume.

With young offenders, facilitators may speak with offenders and their parents together, but it is important to speak with each individually as well. Facilitators need to establish individual rapport with offenders and work to ensure that offenders begin the conference by accepting responsibility for what they did, without rationalizing, minimizing or making excuses.

Accepting responsibility and owning the behavior go beyond a simple admission. In conferences where offenders do not own their behavior, other participants usually become morally indignant, decreasing the chances of successfully reaching a conference agreement. Preparing the offender can avoid this pitfall.

Facilitators prepare offenders during their pre-conference meetings by having them say what happened in their own words. Facilitators should speak to offenders in a positive tone and listen to the offenders tell their stories. Some offenders readily take responsibility for their behavior, saying how sorry they are and that they know it was wrong. In this case, facilitators should offer encouragement and tell offenders that if they speak so humbly and honestly during the conference, the process will probably go very well.

Other offenders make excuses and blame others. When facilitators detect this, they should stop the offender and say something like:

"I want to make sure that this conference goes well for you. I hear you describing what happened and though you've admitted that you did it, you seem to be blaming others, which will just make everyone angry with you. If you have some reasons why things happened the way they did, save them for later in the conference. Just start out really honest and humble, admitting what you did without any explanations. Then the conference will go better. Do you know what I mean? Why don't you try it again, this time just saying what you did and admitting it was wrong."

Facilitators need to establish individual rapport with offenders and work to ensure that offenders begin the conference by accepting responsibility for what they did, without rationalizing, minimizing or making excuses.

Facilitators should listen again and give compliments if the offender seems to be owning the behavior. Facilitators may even tell offenders that people will respond better if they say it the same way during the conference. As a closing statement, facilitators can ask offenders to think about how people have been affected by their actions.

This preparation helps offenders—especially young people who may not have the communication skills to humbly express remorse—start on the right foot in the conference. If an offender's attitude is a deceptive ploy, that will usually become obvious as the conference continues. In most cases, however, offenders are favorably affected by the conference atmosphere and their honesty and positive attitude is reinforced, even if they were not totally sincere at the outset.

During pre-conference meetings, offenders and their parents may rationalize or minimize the offense by blaming other people and situations. Blaming others for the incident often reflects an underlying feeling of shame. For example, sometimes offenders or parents of offenders who assaulted someone may claim that the victim "egged them on" or was "asking for it."

Blaming others for the incident often reflects an underlying feeling of shame.

While there are often other factors that contributed to the offense, facilitators should say that what the offenders did was unacceptable and they need to take responsibility for their part in what happened. Asking questions in the pre-conference meeting such as "If you had it to do over again, what would you do differently?" or "How could you have responded differently?" can help offenders realize they could have chosen less harmful responses.

Parents may have much to say about the incident and the offender, and how they have been personally affected. Facilitators should listen attentively and compassionately, allowing ventilation of feelings and expression of opinions.

Parents of offenders may express anger with the offender. Degrading statements about offenders and their individual worth, such as name-calling and other stigmatizing characterizations, can be dangerous. For example, "John is such a troublemaker" or "Carrie is just like her mother." Facilitators should acknowledge the anger and help the parents explore it, by saying for example, "You seem very angry about what happened. Can you tell me more about that?" There are usually underlying feelings of hurt, disappointment, frustration and shame. Encourage them to express those feelings, rather than characterize the offender as good or bad.

Offenders nominate supporters to be at the conference. The ideal offender supporter is someone whom the offender cares about, who can strongly disapprove of the inappropriate behavior while affirming the offender's positive qualities and worth. When exploring who to invite as offender supporters, facilitators should help the offender think creatively about who is important to them and who can be supportive to them at the conference—including parents, brothers, sisters, extended family, friends, peers, spouses, counselors, coaches, priests, rabbis, neighbors and others. Facilitators can ask offenders, "Who in your life really cares about you?" then ask about people in the different areas of the offenders' life, such as family, school, work, church, clubs and sports. Some offenders have little family support, but might have a social worker, counselor or even probation officer they like and want to have with them at the conference.

Sometimes offenders do not want supporters, usually because they are ashamed for others to know what they did. However, the conference process depends on the inclusion of the offender's "community of care," because offenders are more likely to hear the effects of their actions, acknowledge their shame and express remorse when people that they care about are present. The person the offender seems least comfortable inviting may be the one the facilitator should persuade the offender to invite. Sometimes, particularly in the case of juvenile offenses, parents have every right to attend, and perhaps even extended family members, without the permission of the youth.

When offenders do not readily nominate supporters, facilitators may ask people who know the offender who they think could be a supporter. Even when offenders have no family and friends nearby, there are often people in the community who have had contact with the offenders who can offer support. Conferences help to create or strengthen positive bonds between offenders and people in their community.

If offenders insist that they do not want any supporters at the conference, facilitators should say that

The ideal offender supporter is someone whom the offender cares about, who can strongly disapprove of the inappropriate behavior while affirming the offender's positive qualities and worth.

part of the offenders' positive participation in the conference includes having supporters there, because they offer a special perspective on the offender and can contribute to the conference process and resolution. Facilitators must make it difficult for the offender to refuse supporters.

Before ending the pre-conference meeting, facilitators should address any remaining questions. If they have a tentative time and date for the conference, they should make sure it is acceptable to the offender, but say it may have to be shifted to suit the victim. Facilitators should ask the offender for alternative times. Facilitators should ensure offenders and their parents know how to find the conference site, and possibly offer transportation or provide directions. Lastly facilitators should leave their business card or their written phone number in case offenders or parents need to contact them.

Contacting Victims

The facilitator's primary job in pre-conference meetings with victims is to listen to them relate their feelings and how they were affected by the incident.

When contacting victims, facilitators begin by introducing themselves and explaining the purpose of the conference. For example:

"Hi, my name is (facilitator's name). I'm with (facilitator's agency), and I'm working on setting up a conference dealing with (brief description of offense), in which you were unfortunately harmed. I am organizing a conference to deal with the incident because it can provide you with an opportunity to meet (offender's name), tell (offender's name) how you were affected, ask questions, and have direct involvement in deciding what happens. I'd like to tell you about the conference and answer your questions, so you can decide if you would like to participate. The conference is an alternative to (referring the matter to court/handling the matter through school disciplinary procedures/handling the matter in another way), and most people find it a more satisfying way to repair the harm that has resulted. (Offender's name) has admitted committing the offense and has agreed to participate in the conference. While I can't guarantee what the outcome of the conference will be, I can tell you that it usually goes very well."

Facilitators should explain the conference process, who will be present, what will be asked, and what victims can reasonably expect. Facilitators should describe to victims the potential benefits of the conference process which include: telling the offender how they were affected, holding the offender accountable and having a say in how to repair the harm, possibly receiving an apology and restitution, and asking the offender questions about the offense.

The facilitator's primary job in pre-conference meetings with victims is to listen to them relate their feelings and how they were affected by the incident. Facilitators should allow victims as much time as they need to do this. Even if victims decline participation, or if the conference is not held for some other reason, victims may still appreciate that someone took the time to listen to them—a significant contribution to the healing process.

Facilitators must not pressure victims to participate in a conference. Facilitators can tell victims the advantages of the conference and how other victims have responded to the process. Facilitators should also tell victims if the offenders express a different view about what happened or if offenders seem particularly lacking in remorse. While facilitators should not "sell" the victim on the conference, they can express their enthusiasm for the value of conferencing. If victims decline participation, facilitators should thank them for their consideration.

Victims may nominate anyone they like to support them at the conference. Victims are generally more forthcoming than offenders in nominating supporters, although not always. When victims hesitate to nominate supporters, facilitators should stress that they may feel more comfortable at the conference if they have people to support them. Facilitators should also stress that the victims' family and friends should be at the conference because they have also been affected by the harm done to someone close to them.

Facilitators should check with the victim whether the time, date and location of the conference are convenient. Before ending the meeting, facilitators should answer any remaining questions, provide directions to the conference site if needed, possibly offer transportation, and leave their business card or written phone number in case the victim has additional questions.

Facilitators must not pressure victims to participate in a conference. Facilitators can tell victims the advantages of the conference and how other victims have responded to the process.

Contacting Offender and Victim Supporters

Facilitators should speak with *all* supporters before the conference. Building rapport with supporters increases the chances of a successful conference because they will be more likely to work with the facilitator to see that the process goes well.

When contacting offender and victim supporters, facilitators must introduce themselves, explain the conference process, how the conference will benefit the victim, offender and themselves, and why their participation will be helpful. For example:

"Hi, my name is (facilitator's name). I'm with (facilitator's agency), and I'm working on setting up a conference dealing with (brief description of offense). (Offender's name or victim's name) has asked for you to be at the conference to support them. The conference will help us learn how people have been affected by what happened and how to repair the harm that has resulted. Your presence would benefit the process, and I know (offender's name or victim's name) would like you to attend."

Sometimes supporters know little or nothing about the incident, so facilitators may tell them more about what happened. It may help if victims or offenders contact their nominated supporters to explain the conference and let them know the facilitator will be calling.

Offender and victim supporters may simply see themselves as providing support. Often, however, they have been directly affected by the incident and need to express their feelings—particularly close friends and relatives of victims of more serious crimes. Facilitators should give supporters the same respect and attention as victims, listening and allowing them to discuss their thoughts and feelings.

Like parents of offenders, offender supporters may feel angry and ashamed about what the offender did. Facilitators should re-frame degrading or stigmatizing statements and focus on the underlying feelings of shame, disappointment and hurt.

Before ending the meeting, facilitators should answer any remaining questions, ensure supporters know the conference time, date and location, provide directions to the site if needed, possibly offer transportation,

Building rapport with supporters increases the chances of a successful conference because they will be more likely to work with the facilitator to see that the process goes well.

and leave their business card or written phone number in case the supporters have additional questions.

The Seating Plan

Facilitators should develop a conference seating plan. (See Figure 3 and Figure 4.) In the conference, participants should be seated close together in a circle or oval shape, with no tables or other obstructions in the middle. Tables can inhibit emotional expression because they obscure body language and can be used as protective barriers by participants. The circle also symbolizes community or "coming together."

Participants should be seated close together in a circle or oval shape, with no tables or other obstructions in the middle.

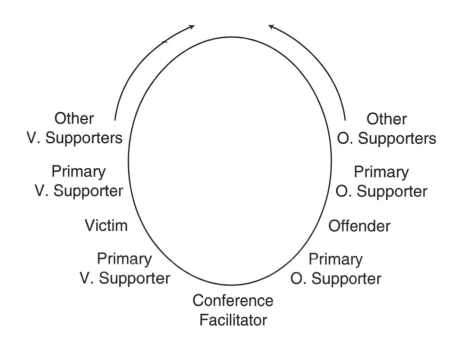

Figure 3: Conference Seating Guide

Offenders and their supporters should sit in the circle on one side of the facilitator, and victims and their supporters should sit in the circle on the other side of the facilitator. The offender group generally sits on the right and the victim group on the left. This is arbitrary, but facilitators should adopt one approach—offender right/victim left *or* offender left/victim right—and stick with it over time to help them manage their conferences more smoothly.

Offenders and victims should sit next to their closest supporters and near, but not necessarily next to, the facilitator. For young offenders, their closest supporters

Figure 4

Conference Seating Planner

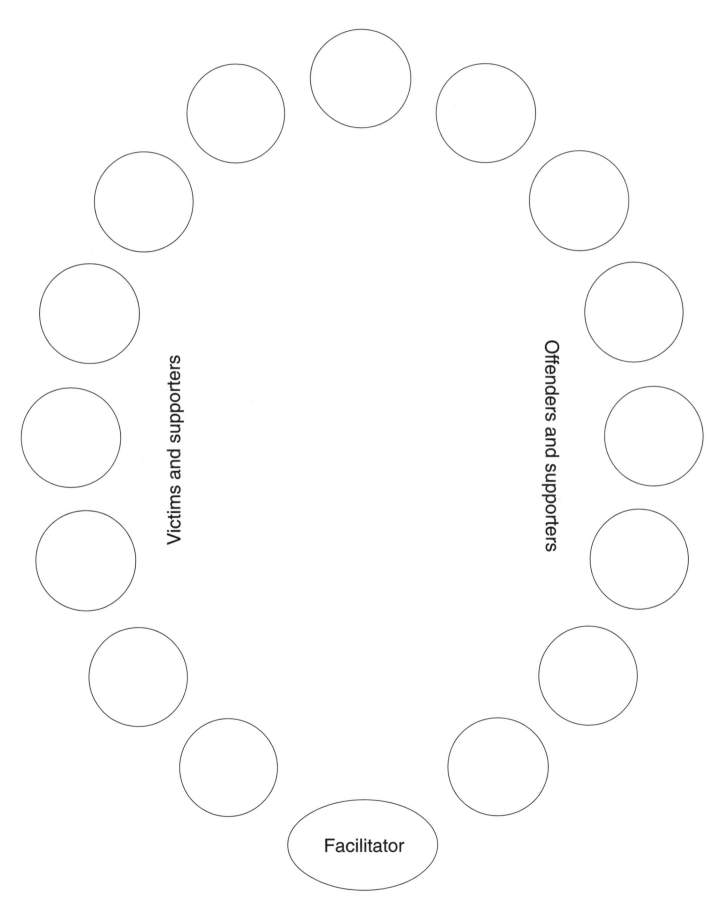

are usually parents or guardians, who can sit to either side. If there are multiple offenders, each should sit between their closest supporters.

Other victim supporters and offender supporters should sit on their respective sides of the circle, with both groups' seating progressing away from the facilitator toward the point in the circle opposite the facilitator.

Participants who are not explicitly a victim or offender supporter, such as an investigating police officer, can be seated between the two groups, opposite the facilitator. If facilitators feel that a particular participant may be disruptive or troublesome in the conference, they may choose to seat that participant nearest to them to make it more uncomfortable for that person to be disruptive.

Offenders and victims should sit next to their closest supporters.

Large Conferences

On the rare occasion when a conference is particularly large, perhaps 30 or more people, facilitators should arrange participants in rows of chairs, with victims and their supporters facing offenders and their supporters and the facilitator seated between the two groups, as in Figure 5 below.

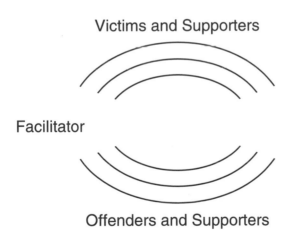

Figure 5: Large Conference Diagram

Because of the time and number of people involved in large conferences, facilitators will need help seating people, answering questions, taking care of unexpected problems, and guiding people to restrooms and refreshments—which should be available throughout the conference. The assistant or co-facilitator may chat with people when they have refreshments and encourage them to return to the conference because some may be discouraged by the length. A large pad of paper, easel and marker are useful for constructing the conference agreement.

Additional Preparation

Facilitators should envision how the conference may unfold. This becomes easier as facilitators gain experience and understanding of the dynamics of conferences. Their trust in the process will grow as well.

Each conference is unique, but patterns emerge that help facilitators organize and prepare. For instance, if the offender readily takes responsibility in the start of the conference, victims and others are less likely to express moral indignation. Or if the offender's parents are harsh with the offender, other participants may say something positive or supportive about the offender.

Each facilitator will develop a way of organizing conference preparation materials. Facilitators should record the phone numbers and addresses of conference participants and other relevant contacts. They may also keep notes on their discussions with conference participants and others to review during conference preparation or for later reference.

Facilitators should be familiar with the conference script, and read through it to determine the order that participants will speak, noting the order on the script or seating plan. Labels with participants' names can be placed on the seats before participants arrive. Facilitators should ensure the conference room is reserved and that all participants were told the correct time, date and location of the conference. Facilitators may put a sign on the door saying, "Do Not Disturb: Conference In Progress." Also, facilitators will provide tissues, which signify to participants that emotional expression is acceptable, and refreshments for the informal period after the conference.

If facilitators are concerned about handling a particular situation, they should seek advice from a colleague who has been trained in facilitating Real Justice conferences. Real Justice provides direct support for facilitators, free of charge, via telephone and email.

Facilitators should envision how the conference may unfold. This becomes easier as facilitators gain experience and understanding of the dynamics of conferences. Their trust in the process will grow as well.

Facilitators who have been trained by Real Justice may also join "RealJustice-Talk," an internet discussion group for facilitators throughout the world.

Real Justice provides direct support for facilitators, free of charge, via telephone and email.

Facilitator's Preparation Checklist

❏ Do you have a clear understanding of the incident?

❏ Is a conference needed?

❏ Has the offender admitted responsibility?

❏ Have you invited all necessary participants?

❏ Have you spoken or met with *all* participants and secured their attendance?

❏ Do participants understand the conference process and its purpose?

❏ Do participants know how to contact you?

❏ Have you reserved a suitable room?

❏ Do participants know the time, date and location, and how to get there?

❏ Do participants have transportation?

❏ Have you developed a seating plan?

❏ Are you familiar with the conference facilitator's script?

❏ Have you thought about how the conference may unfold?

❏ Do you need assistance, a co-facilitator or an observer to give you feedback?

❏ Do you know what may happen if the conference does not reach an agreement or the offender fails to satisfy the agreement?

❏ Do you have the following items for the conference?
   - ❏ a copy of the conference facilitator's script
   - ❏ agreement forms and other required forms
   - ❏ the conference seating plan
   - ❏ participant seating labels
   - ❏ a "Do Not Disturb" sign
   - ❏ a box of tissues
   - ❏ refreshments

Chapter 4: Running the Conference

Before the Conference

Before participants arrive, facilitators set up the conference room, arranging chairs according to the seating plan and taking into account any last-minute changes. There should be no tables or other physical obstructions within the circle of chairs. Labels with participants' names may be placed on the chairs to help the seating process. Facilitators should bring their conference script (photocopied from pages 18-20 of this manual), agreement forms, seating plan, a box of tissues, and refreshments for the informal period after the conference.

The room should be free from noise and visual distractions, such as a window looking out onto a busy street. If there is a phone or intercom in the room, the ringer should be turned off. A "Do Not Disturb: Conference In Progress" sign may be placed on doors accessing the room. Facilitators should locate the nearest restrooms so they can direct participants to them. Facilitators also need access to a photocopier to duplicate the conference agreement after it is signed.

If possible, there should be separate waiting areas for victims and their supporters and offenders and their supporters to avoid the mutual discomfort of facing each other in silence before the conference convenes. When participants arrive, the facilitator should meet them and direct them to a waiting area. Facilitators should be courteous and respectful, and maintain the formality and seriousness of the occasion. An assistant may help facilitators greet and direct participants. Facilitators should keep track of who has arrived.

Sometimes facilitators meet with each group separately, just before the conference, to review the conference process, address last-minute questions or concerns, and explain the seating arrangements. This is optional.

Setting Up
Before the Conference:

- *Have conference script, forms, seating plan, tissues, refreshments*
- *Chairs arranged according to seating plan*
- *No tables or physical obstructions within circle*
- *Labels with participants' names on chairs*
- *Room free from distractions*
- *Ringer turned off on phone or intercom*
- *"Do Not Disturb" sign on doors*
- *Restrooms located*
- *Copy machine accessible*
- *Waiting areas for victims' group and offenders' group*

If an offender, victim or key supporter is late, facilitators should wait a reasonable amount of time, perhaps telephoning the individual. If there is one offender or one victim, and either does not show up to the conference, the conference should be re-scheduled if possible. If it seems that a full conference will not occur, a modified conference may address the needs of the people who have been assembled.

If a peripheral supporter has not arrived, facilitators may wait a short time and then begin the conference. It is not a good idea to admit participants once the conference has begun. Their perspective will differ from other participants who have experienced the conference from the beginning. Facilitators may allow late-comers to observe the conference from outside the circle or participate in some limited way, depending on when they arrive.

If victims or offenders bring unexpected supporters, facilitators usually allow them to participate. However, facilitators should speak with them about the conference process and purpose, and tell them what they will be asked in the conference. If it appears the unexpected supporters are indignant and may sabotage the conference process—on purpose or inadvertently—facilitators should speak with them further. Facilitators should explain that much preparation has gone into the conference, that all who came to the conference took time from their days and are invested in the conference going well, and that they are welcome to participate in a respectful and constructive manner.

If an offender comes without supporters, facilitators may choose not to conference, re-schedule, or confer with victims and others about whether to proceed.

If a participant is obviously intoxicated, they should not participate, out of respect for the rest of the participants. If facilitators merely suspect that a participant is intoxicated, they should rely on their judgment to determine if that person will be disruptive, monitor them during the conference, and ask them to leave later if they behave inappropriately.

To begin the conference, facilitators bring one group into the conference room at a time, preferably the victim's group first. When everyone is seated, the facilitator begins the conference. There should generally be no interruptions after starting.

If it seems that a full conference will not occur, a modified conference may address the needs of the people who have been assembled.

Facilitators should have a clipboard or folder with the seating plan, the conference script, blank paper for developing the conference agreement, and agreement forms or other forms to be completed.

Throughout the conference, facilitators should be calm, take their time, speak evenly and allow silence between speakers and questions. They should always be respectful, especially when responding to a challenge. Facilitators should never express personal opinions about the incident or make suggestions. However, as guardians of the conference process, they must be ready to assert themselves with participants who stray from the conference focus or otherwise disrupt the process.

Below is a description of the conference script and its phases. Sections from the script are indented and in a different typeface.

The Preamble

Facilitators begin the conference by welcoming everyone, introducing themselves and then participants, saying their names and stating their relationships to the offender or victim.

1. Preamble

> **"Welcome. As you know, my name is** (your name) **and I will be facilitating this conference."**

> Now introduce each conference participant and state his/ her relationship to the offender/s or victim/s.

For the introductions, facilitators will generally state each person's first and last names. Facilitators should never use the terms "offender" and "victim" to describe individuals during the conference. Depending on the setting, the age and status of the participants, facilitators may also include prefixes or titles instead of or in addition to first names, such as "Mr./Mrs./Ms./Dr.," "officer" or "principal." For example:

"This is Chris Rogers, whose behavior we are here to discuss today. This is Steve Rogers, Chris's father and Laura Rogers, Chris's sister. This is Bob Reading, Chris's basketball coach. This is Officer Johnson, who conducted

Throughout the conference, facilitators should be calm, take their time, speak evenly and allow silence between speakers and questions.

Facilitators should never express personal opinions about the incident or make suggestions.

the initial investigation and made the arrest. This is Mary Huang, whose car tires were slashed by Chris, and this is Mary's husband, John Huang. And lastly, this is Cindy Smith, Mary's friend."

How facilitators introduce participants frames their roles in the conference. It may help to reiterate each participant's relationship to the victim or offender the first couple of times they are addressed. For example, "Let's speak now with Bob Reading, Chris's basketball Coach. Mr. Reading, what did you think when you heard about the incident?"

After introducing participants, facilitators should thank everyone for attending and set the conference focus—to explore how people have been affected by the incident and how to repair the harm that has resulted. The description of the incident should be brief.

> **"Thank you all for attending. I know that this is difficult for all of you, but your presence will help us deal with the matter that has brought us together. This is an opportunity for all of you to be involved in repairing the harm that has been done."**

> **"This conference will focus on an incident which happened** (state the date, place and nature of offense without elaborating)**. It is important to understand that we will focus on what** (offender name/s) **did and how that unacceptable behavior has affected others. We are not here to decide whether** (offender name/s) **is/are good or bad. We want to explore in what way people have been affected and hopefully work toward repairing the harm that has resulted. Does everyone understand this?"**

During the conference, facilitators can re-state the focus when participants are off-track.

The conference focus tells participants what will happen without prescribing the outcome. During the conference, facilitators can re-state the focus when participants are off-track. If a participant calls the offender names or uses stigmatizing or degrading language, the facilitator can re-state a phrase from the preamble: "We are not here to decide whether (offender name / s) is good or bad. We want to explore in what way people have been affected . . ." Repeating portions of the preamble reminds people of the intended tone and purpose of the conference and allows the facilitator to avoid direct confrontation with participants. They tend to honor this re-direction because they already have a positive rapport with the facilitator.

After setting the focus, facilitators should remind offenders, as well as other participants, that they have the right to leave the conference. Offenders must acknowledge that if they do leave, the incident may be handled in a different way, perhaps through a formal judicial or disciplinary process.

"(Offender name/s) **has**/have **admitted his**/her/their **part in the incident.**"

Say to offender/s: "**I must tell you that you do not have to participate in this conference and are free to leave at any time, as is anyone else. If you do leave, the matter may be referred to court**/handled by the school disciplinary policy/ handled in another way."

"**This matter, however, may be finalized if you participate in a positive manner and comply with the conference agreement.**"

Say to offender/s: "**Do you understand?**"

This portion of the script was initially added to safeguard the offenders' right to due process in the criminal justice system. Facilitators might also ask the parents of young offenders to acknowledge their children's rights as well. The phrase "as is anyone else" was added later to clarify that all participants have the right to leave at any time.

In addition to admitting responsibility for the offense, offenders are expected to participate in the conference in a positive manner and carry out commitments they make in the conference.

Offenders are expected to participate in the conference in a positive manner and carry out commitments they make in the conference.

Speaking With Offenders

Offenders are asked to speak before the victims or any other participants in the conference. A consensus has developed among experienced conference facilitators that having offenders speak first is beneficial to victims and the whole conference process. This consensus is supported by studies showing high rates of victim satisfaction with the conferencing process.

Many victims have said that they would prefer for offenders to go first, rather than be put "on the spot." More often than not, the offenders take responsibility for the offense in a way that reduces victims' anger, anxiety and moral indignation—thereby saving victims a great deal of unpleasantness.

Offenders speaking first eliminates false preconceptions among participants about the offender's attitude, allowing a more informed and realistic exchange. Defensiveness from the offenders' parents and other supporters can be avoided if they hear what the offenders have done, in the offenders' own words.

If offenders refuse responsibility, the facilitator should address this immediately. The facilitator and the participants may decide not to proceed with the conference. If the conference does proceed, participants can take the offender's attitude into account.

Clarifying the offender's attitude up front allows the conference to move toward more satisfying and useful activities—exploring how people were affected and repairing harm. Also, if victims and other participants were to start the conference by verbally attacking an offender who is already predisposed to take appropriate responsibility, the process would be unnecessarily complicated.

2. Offender/s

"We'll start with (one of offenders' names)**."**

If there is more than one offender, have each respond to all of the following questions.

- **"What happened?"**
- **"What were you thinking about at the time?"**

A consensus has developed among experienced conference facilitators that having offenders speak first is beneficial to victims and the whole conference process.

If offenders refuse responsibility, the facilitator should address this immediately.

• "What have you thought about since the incident?"
• "Who do you think has been affected by your actions?"
• "How have they been affected?"

When there are multiple offenders, facilitators may ask each offender every question, one offender at a time. Depending on their experience and comfort level, facilitators may alternate between offenders. This gives all offenders equal opportunity to take responsibility early in the conference. It can build a fuller picture of what happened and help address any discrepancies between the offenders' stories.

Some offenders will give short answers, leave out details, or find it difficult to speak at all. Facilitators should allow extended silence, so offenders can think about what to say and know that the facilitator is not just going to move on if they do not answer. Silence is a powerful tool for overcoming an offender's passive resistance. In a respectful way, silence makes it uncomfortable for the offender to stay aloof from the conference. It is OK for offenders to feel uncomfortable. After a period of silence, the facilitator may re-state the question.

Follow-up or clarifying questions may be necessary, particularly when offenders are describing what happened. Some follow-up questions might be: "Could you tell us more about that?" "What did you do after that?" "What happened next?"

Facilitators should not worry about small discrepancies in facts, nor should they rigorously challenge offenders on their statements. Offenders need not fill in every single detail of the offense, the events leading up to it and afterward. However, they should clearly state their roles and responsibility, without making excuses or blaming others.

Despite follow-up questions and extended silences, some offenders may say little or take little responsibility. Other participants may spontaneously confront or ask questions of the offender. Facilitators should allow this as long as the discussion stays on track. If the discussion moves off focus, the facilitator should re-state the language from the preamble that describes

Silence is a powerful tool for overcoming an offender's passive resistance.

The decision to end a conference is rare and should be exercised with caution.

the conference focus, ask the offender another question, or if the offender has already answered all five questions, move on.

If offenders deny the offense, the facilitator may say that a condition for holding the conference was that the offenders admitted their part in the incident, but now thcy arc denying it. Facilitators can remind offenders about what they said during a pre-conference meeting. If offenders continue to deny responsibility, the facilitator may stop the conference, or allow participants to discuss whether they want to continue.

If participants, especially victims, want to continue despite the offenders' denial, and the offender chooses to stay, the facilitator can allow it. Offenders may reverse their denial, or participants may "agree to disagree," figuring that despite the differences in people's versions of the facts, something can still be gained from the conference. However, if an impasse is reached that cannot be resolved after a reasonable amount of discussion, the conference should be ended. The decision to end a conference is rare and should be exercised with caution.

Sometimes other conference participants will shift the blame for the offense. Parents may blame the school for not properly supervising their child. The offender and victim groups may unite and blame the police or the school for mishandling the situation. While these situations are rare, if facilitators have adequate rapport with participants they can be dealt with by refocusing the discussion. If participants continue to shift blame, the facilitator may allow a limited time to address the issue, particularly if the "accused" party is present. If participants do not move beyond this stance, even after lengthy discussion, the facilitator should end the conference.

Occasionally offenders in conferences may smile or otherwise act inappropriately. While this is probably due to anxiety or a lack of social skills, other participants may see the behavior as contemptuous or defiant. If necessary, facilitators can intervene by asking offenders about their behavior, whether they realized what they were doing, or by asking their parents or other offender supporters to interpret the behavior.

Speaking With Victims

Having victims and their supporters speak before the offender supporters further confronts the offender group with the reality of what the offender has done, helping to avoid potential defensiveness and rationalization of the offenders' behavior. When offenders are done speaking, facilitators should cue victims to speak. Facilitators can precede their questions with a statement such as "Now let's find out from (name of victim) how he/she has been affected."

3. Victim/s

If there is more than one victim, have each respond to all of the following questions.

- **"What was your reaction at the time of the incident?"**
- **"How do you feel about what happened?"**
- **"What has been the hardest thing for you?"**
- **"How did your family and friends react when they heard about the incident?"**

Facilitators should again allow plenty of time and silence for victims to think and respond to questions. For their first few conferences, facilitators should simply ask all four questions in the suggested order. With some experience, facilitators may decide to skip a question if it has already been fully answered. This should be an exception, rather than a rule. A differently phrased question—even if it has already been answered—can elicit a different response or an elaboration.

Victims are generally forthcoming in describing their thoughts and feelings. Their responses will depend on what the offenders said and how they perceive the offenders. If the offenders show remorse and appropriate responsibility, victims may be more understanding and sometimes are remarkably generous.

If the offenders have failed to take responsibility or show remorse, victims may understandably display moral indignation. Facilitators should allow victims to vent their feelings. On the rare occasion when a victim verbally abuses the offender, the facilitator may

Having victims and their supporters speak before the offender supporters further confronts the offender group with the reality of what the offender has done.

Victims may directly ask the offender questions, which the facilitator should allow.

respectfully remind the victim that "we are here to learn how everyone has been affected, but please let's not call each other names."

If a victim has difficulty speaking, facilitators can allow the victim time to respond or regain composure, or possibly move on to others and get back to that victim later.

Victims may directly ask the offender questions, which the facilitator should allow. Victims often want to know why offenders committed the offense, why the offenders chose them to victimize, and want to be assured it will not happen again. If the offender was not forthcoming or remorseful, victims may have many challenging questions.

Speaking With Victim Supporters

When it seems that victims have fully responded to the questions and are finished speaking, facilitators should begin questioning the victim supporters. The victim's closest supporters should be asked to speak first.

4. Victim Supporters

Have each respond to all of the following questions.

• **"What did you think when you heard about the incident?"**
• **"How do you feel about what happened?"**
• **"What has been the hardest thing for you?"**
• **"What do you think are the main issues?"**

Facilitators should allow plenty of time for participants to respond to questions. As with victims, victim supporters' responses will depend on the offenders' apparent attitude, acceptance of responsibility and level of remorse.

Some participants may interact spontaneously. Facilitators can allow this, but should ensure that each participant has the opportunity to fully answer all questions. Facilitators can let the discussion go for a time, and then re-focus by asking the next question from the script. When the victim supporters have spoken, facilitators should move to the offender supporters.

Speaking With Offender Supporters

The first offender supporter the facilitator questions should have the strongest attachment to the offender and be most likely to exhibit the strongest emotional response. If the offender is a youth, this is usually the offender's mother. The facilitator should say, "This has been difficult for you, hasn't it? Would you like to tell us about it?" before asking the remaining four questions from the script.

5. Offender Supporters

To parent/caregiver ask: **"This has been difficult for you, hasn't it? Would you like to tell us about it?"**

Have each respond to all of the following questions.

- **"What did you think when you heard about the incident?"**
- **"How do you feel about what happened?"**
- **"What has been the hardest thing for you?"**
- **"What do you think are the main issues?"**

Continuing with the next closest in relation to the offender, other offender supporters should then be asked these last four questions. Sometimes participants interact spontaneously, and facilitators should ensure that each participant has an opportunity to speak. Usually participants will wait until they are directly addressed.

Parents of offenders often express intense feelings of distress and shame. Facilitators should allow silences and not rush to the next part of the script. Offender supporters are primary triggers of the offenders' shame and remorse about their wrongdoing.

Offender supporters sometimes defend or rationalize what the offender did. This can undermine the conference and diminish the significance of the harm the offender caused. Facilitators may re-focus the conference by re-stating part of the preamble.

More often, offender supporters will try to show remorse by taking a tough stance against the offender.

The first offender supporter the facilitator questions should have the strongest attachment to the offender and be most likely to exhibit the strongest emotional response.

Offender supporters are primary triggers of the offenders' shame and remorse about their wrongdoing.

If this manifests itself as stigmatizing or degrading statements toward the offender, the facilitator may intervene. Other participants, including victims and their supporters, may re-focus the discussion before the facilitator needs to act.

Offender supporters sometimes say they were surprised or shocked or disappointed by what the offender did. This is an opportunity to help offender supporters make the distinction between the offense and the offender. The facilitator can ask them why they felt that way. They may make statements such as "because he is normally a good kid" or "because she usually doesn't act that way." These statements show that while the offense was inappropriate, the offender does have good qualities.

The Agreement Phase

When all participants have spoken, participants may continue to interact. They will often turn to issues of reparation and apology on their own. To help the process of reparation, the facilitator should—at some appropriate point—ask the next question from the script.

6. Offender/s

Ask the offender/s: **"Is there anything you want to say at this time?"**

Sometimes offenders may have nothing to say. Often, however, they will apologize to victims, their family and others in the conference. Next the facilitator should ask the victims what they would like from the conference, involving offenders and the rest of the conference participants in the process of creating a conference agreement.

7. Reaching an Agreement

Ask the victim/s: **"What would you like from today's conference?"**

Ask the offender/s to respond.

The agreement phase is the least structured part of the conference. Participants freely discuss their ideas for how to repair the harm.

At this point, the participants discuss what should be in the final agreement. Solicit comments from participants.

It is important that you ask the offender/s to respond to each suggestion before the group moves to the next suggestion, asking **"What do you think about that?"** Then determine that the offender/s agree/s before moving on. Allow for negotiation.

As the agreement develops, clarify each item and make the written document as specific as possible, including details, deadlines and follow-up arrangements.

As you sense that the agreement discussion is drawing to a close, say to the participants:
"Before I prepare the written agreement, I'd like to make sure that I have accurately recorded what has been decided."

Read the items in the agreement aloud and look to the participants for acknowledgment. Make any necessary corrections.

The agreement phase is the least structured part of the conference. Participants freely discuss their ideas for how to repair the harm. The facilitator clarifies and records items accurately and in detail, checks with the victim, offender and other participants that they are OK with each item, and monitors discussions to ensure participants stay focused. Facilitators should encourage a variety of ideas and allow plenty of time for discussion. If discussion is limited, facilitators may canvas participants for their suggestions and comments.

Most conferences lead to a mutually acceptable agreement. The ultimate decision to include an item in the agreement is the offender's and the victim's. Typically the conference agreement is written during the conference and signed by victims, offenders and parents of young offenders, or perhaps by all participants, shortly after the conference. On rare occasions conferences may simply result in a spoken understanding among participants. Conference outcomes vary greatly, depending on the circumstances of the offense, the needs

The ultimate decision to include an item in the agreement is the offender's and the victim's.

of the participants, and the offenders' attitude in the conference.

Facilitators should not impose their opinions or suggestions on the conference agreement. For instance, they should not recommend that every offender complete community service. If participants decide that community service is appropriate, facilitators may then provide information on community service options.

On rare occasions when facilitators feel that items in the agreement are unreasonable, harsh, or that there is an excessive number of conditions, facilitators may "reality test" by tactfully asking if participants have similar concerns. If everyone, including the offender, is comfortable with the agreement as it stands, then the facilitator should defer.

If the agreement includes personal service by offenders for the victim, facilitators should make sure that victims are comfortable with this. Victims may ask a conference participant to accompany the offender when they do the task.

Genuine apology and forgiveness is voluntarily and spontaneously offered, not coerced.

Facilitators should never imply or suggest that offenders apologize, nor should they encourage victims to forgive offenders. Genuine apology and forgiveness is voluntarily and spontaneously offered, not coerced.

Sometimes all victims want is a spoken or written apology. Facilitators should *never* insist that offenders do more than the participants have agreed to, even if they think the offender is getting off easy. Symbolic reparation—apology, forgiveness, reintegration—is usually more satisfying for participants than material reparation. The outcome of the conference belongs to the participants.

Plans for monetary restitution or service should include exact amounts and schedules for completion, and specify who will supervise and monitor the agreements.

Plans for monetary restitution or service should include exact amounts and schedules for completion, and specify who will supervise and monitor the agreements. Ideally monitors should be conference participants, not the facilitator or other professionals. A plan for what should happen if the offender fails to complete the agreement might also be included.

Closing the Conference

Before closing, facilitators should ensure that all participants had a chance to express themselves. After the agreement is finalized and before formally closing the conference, facilitators should give everyone a final opportunity to speak. Facilitators should then thank participants for their contributions, invite them to have refreshments, and ask them to stay until they have signed the written conference agreement.

8. Closing the Conference

"Before I formally close this conference, I would like to provide everyone with a final opportunity to speak. Is there anything anyone wants to say?"

Allow for participants to respond and when they are done, say:

"Thank you for your contributions in dealing with this difficult matter. Congratulations on the way you have worked through the issues. Please help yourselves to some refreshments while I prepare the agreement."

Allow participants ample time to have refreshments and interact. The informal period after the formal conference is very important.

The informal period after the conference, when refreshments are served, is critical to the conference process. It should never be omitted. Much reintegration can occur during this time. Participants generally feel relief that the difficult conference process is over and even satisfaction and enjoyment that they successfully developed and agreed upon a plan to repair the harm.

Refreshments need not be elaborate. For the typical conference, a cold beverage and pretzels or cookies should suffice. In very large conferences which tend to run longer, the facilitator should probably add something more substantial, such as coffee and pastries.

Facilitators should complete the conference agreement, obtain signatures from the necessary participants, and give copies of the agreement to everyone who needs one. Facilitators should say good-bye to all participants as they leave and thank them again for their participation.

The informal period after the conference, when refreshments are served, is critical to the conference process.

Other Points About Facilitating Conferences

Surprises. Occasionally an unexpected revelation occurs. For example, someone may say that they have been sexually abused, or the offender may disclose that they have committed other offenses. When the revelation is particularly serious and overshadows the conference, the facilitator should stop the conference. In other cases, it may be sufficient to acknowledge the revelation and continue.

If the facilitator is a police officer and a serious offense is revealed in the conference, by either the offender in the conference or by another participant, the officer needs to recognize that person's legal rights. Other facilitators may need to contact the police about the offense. In many jurisdictions where there are laws governing mediation and alternative dispute resolution, disclosures made during a conference will not be admissible in court. Facilitators should know their local laws. However, these laws may not have been adequately tested in the courts.

Varying from the script. While facilitators are advised to stay with the script, within that framework there are occasions when facilitators must improvise. In general, facilitators should speak simply and clearly, avoiding bureaucratic, legalistic or professional jargon. Facilitators should never condescend or patronize, and should avoid mimicking the mannerisms and expressions of participants. When facilitators need to paraphrase questions to help someone understand what is being asked, they should ask open-ended questions which elicit more than a "multiple choice" or "yes or no" answer.

Allowing for emotion. Conference participants should be free to express the full range of emotions. While this may feel uncomfortable at times, it is absolutely necessary for successful conferences. No "ground rules," per se, are established at the beginning of the conference. Ground rules about not raising one's voice or not saying anything negative about someone can deny participants the opportunity to deal with their legitimate anger and constrain how they express themselves.

Only when emotions are expressed in a stigmatizing or abusive way should facilitators intervene. Facilitators

> **Conference participants should be free to express the full range of emotions. Only when emotions are expressed in a stigmatizing or abusive way should facilitators intervene.**

should not be too quick to re-focus the discussion, however, because other participants may intervene first.

Facilitators should allow substantial time for participants to express their thoughts and feelings and should not avoid or intervene in highly emotional exchanges. Some participants may cry, a natural response to a distressing situation. Crying can greatly impact the offender and others in the conference. When a person is crying, the facilitator should allow silence and can quietly offer that person a tissue.

Re-directing eye contact. Often participants will speak directly to facilitators when answering questions, inhibiting group interaction. To discourage this, facilitators can look at their scripts or other participants. For example, if an offender expresses remorse about the offense, the facilitator can look at the victim to encourage the offender to address that victim.

Inappropriate signs of approval. When questioning participants, facilitators may be tempted to nod their heads in support. Others may see this as approval or agreement and think the facilitator is partial. Therefore, facilitators should avoid nodding their heads when participants speak.

Laughter and humor. Participants may sometimes laugh or joke. As with other emotional expressions, laughter can be appropriate in a conference, often bringing participants a sense of relief.

Profanity. Sometimes conference participants will use profanity, usually in anger. In general, facilitators should not worry about this. However, if the language persists and is abusive or offensive to others, the facilitator may intervene if others do not.

Use of silence. Silence is powerful. Silence emphasizes the impact of comments, allows participants to reflect, enables facilitators to collect their thoughts or determine how to re-focus discussion, permits participants to regain their composure, and shifts the emphasis toward non-verbal communication.

Translators in conferences. Sometimes a participant may speak little or no English. Facilitators can enlist that participant's relative or friend or a neutral third party to translate. Facilitators should allow extra time between questions for translation.

Arranging further services for participants. Conference participants sometimes bring up problems or issues not

Facilitators should avoid nodding their heads when participants are speaking.

directly related to the incident or requiring more substantial attention than the conference can provide. Depending on the setting and the facilitators' experience, facilitators may recommend and refer conference participants to services addressing these issues. Facilitators may even know how to obtain financial support for such services. It is usually best for facilitators to offer referrals outside the formal conference, perhaps during a pre-conference meeting or after the conference. This ensures that facilitators will not be seen as an ally of a particular person or group.

Chapter 5: Establishing a Conferencing Program

Getting Trained

While some will facilitate a conference (or a modified version) after hearing the process described, and others will try conferencing after reading this handbook, most want formal training first.

Real Justice offers a two-day conference facilitator training with videos, role plays and books (including this handbook). Trainees see conferences on videotape, facilitate a role-played conference using the script, participate in several role plays, and experience different conference roles—victim, victim supporter, offender, offender supporter. Trainees can also ask questions and get answers from experienced trainers who have facilitated conferences.

Start Facilitating Conferences

To establish a conference program, individuals should start by facilitating a conference, picking one case or incident and simply taking the risk. Recently-trained facilitators should run a conference within 30 days of the training, while the experience is fresh in their minds. First-time facilitators commonly report that "it was a textbook conference" because they usually go well. For the unfortunate few who have a less positive experience in their first conferences, the next will likely be "textbook."

If a group from the same organization attends a training, the first to facilitate a conference inspires others to do the same. Group members can sit in on each other's conferences, as observers outside the circle, and provide constructive feedback.

After doing several conferences, facilitators may invite others from their organization, particularly the leadership, to sit in and observe an actual conference. Showing people an actual conference is the best way to overcome their resistance. When an observer attends,

Real Justice offers a two-day conference facilitator training with videos, role plays and books.

Showing people an actual conference is the best way to overcome their resistance.

facilitators should tell participants who the observer is and ask if they object. Almost invariably participants will not object.

Defining the Program

The program should now be more clearly defined. Some questions to be answered include:
- Who will refer cases to be conferenced?
- Which cases should be conferenced?
- What criteria will be applied?
- How will cases be referred and tracked?
- What are the parameters?
- Who will facilitate the conferences?
- How will the flow of cases be managed?
- Who will monitor the agreements?

This handbook cannot answer these questions because they depend on the organization, setting, political climate and many other variables. For help with these issues, program organizers can contact the Real Justice office or use the "RealJustice-Talk" email group to converse with others who have set up a conferencing program.

Handling Participant Refusals

Because conferencing is voluntary, one or more potential participants may refuse to participate. When they are not critical to the conference, it can proceed. When the primary victim or offender decline, some programs ask them to participate instead in a hearing or panel proceeding. When the primary victim declines participation, facilitators may hold a conference with offenders, their supporters and secondary victims.

Ideally, hearings or panel proceedings will incorporate many elements of a restorative process. The hearing officer or panel members can ask the offender, the victim and others questions normally asked in a conference, fostering many of the same dynamics and outcomes.

Program Literature

Appendix II includes literature and forms from several conferencing programs. The literature—which includes informational brochures, letters to participants, participant questionnaires, agreement forms, facilitator guidelines and consent forms—will help those developing conferencing programs. Facilitators in these programs use the scripted model of conferencing and, with the exception of the Wagga Wagga Police Patrol, have been trained by Real Justice.

Programs need not develop prepared agreement forms or any of the specific pieces of literature offered in this chapter. These are merely examples of how particular programs have implemented conferencing in their settings.

Wagga Wagga Police Patrol. The first sample (page 98) is the conference agreement form used by police in Wagga Wagga, New South Wales, Australia, where scripted conferencing originated. Conferences were called "cautioning conferences" because they were held as an alternative to the traditional formal police "caution" or warning. The statement on the agreement form, "My family and I will complete the following undertaking/s . . ." illustrates that the offender's family was seen as responsible for monitoring the offender's completion of the agreement.

Central Bucks School District. The next sample (pages 99-100) is an informational pamphlet from Central Bucks School District, Pennsylvania, explaining what "family group conferencing" is, its goals, who is involved, and how people benefit from the process. Central Bucks has been using conferencing district-wide in elementary, middle and high schools. They emphasize the importance of maintaining a sense of safety and a positive learning environment.

Central City Neighborhoods Partnership. The Central City Neighborhoods Partnership (CCNP) is a community-based conferencing program in Minneapolis addressing "quality-of-life" crimes—crimes that contribute to the deterioration of neighborhoods—committed by adults. Offenses addressed include soliciting prostitution, trespassing, public alcohol consumption, public urination, disorderly conduct, vandalism, panhandling, shoplifting and theft.

The conferencing model used by CCNP differs from the standard Real Justice model by including community members in conferences who represent the interests of the neighborhood as a whole. Also, the program establishes "ground rules" for conferences in addition to the conference focus set forth in the script, and requires that the conference agreement specifically includes a plan to "restore the victim if there is a direct victim" and "make amends to the community."

Included here is a variety of materials from CCNP:

- Reparative agreement form (pages 101-102)
- Program pamphlet to describe the program and recruit community volunteers (pages 103-104)
- Evaluation forms for the facilitator, offenders, victims and community participants, offender supporters, victim supporters and "third party participants" (pages 105-111)
- Pre-meeting checklist, used when meeting with participants as preparation for the conference (pages 112-113)
- Program newsletter distributed to community members (pages 114-117)

Hawke's Bay Restorative Justice Te Puna Wai Ora Inc. While New Zealand's government has implemented conferencing on a national scale for young offenders, this local volunteer program provides conferencing for adult offenses.

Materials include:

- Code of practice for facilitators and the management committee, which oversees the program and supports facilitators (page 118)
- Complaints procedure for anyone involved in conferences to issue a complaint about the conference process or outcome (page 119)
- Code of ethics for facilitators (page 120)
- Referral protocols, basic guidelines for referring cases to conferencing (page 121)
- Report form to record the conference outcomes and follow-up plan (page 122)
- General information pamphlet (pages 123-124)
- Conference participant pamphlet, which includes a statement of participants' rights and responsibilities (pages 125-126)
- Procedural guidelines for making conference arrangements, professional practices and management responsibilities (pages 127-128)

Piedmont Dispute Resolution Center. The Piedmont Dispute Resolution Center is a community-based, non-profit organization in Warrenton, Virginia, which receives juvenile case referrals from courts and schools. A staff conference coordinator manages the conferencing program, keeps track of case referrals and dispositions, and supervises and assigns cases to a team of volunteer conference facilitators.

Materials include:

- Agreement form (page 129)
- Flowchart depicting case flow from referral to conference (page 130)
- Flowchart depicting case flow from conference to outcome (page 131)
- Information release consent to permit the Piedmont Dispute Resolution Center to receive confidential information regarding the case (page 132)
- Information sheet providing a basic description of the conferencing program (page 133)
- Conferencing consent form which participants sign to indicate that they understand the role of the facilitator, the right to choose another alternative such as court, the confidentiality of the proceedings, and their obligation to carry out the conference agreement (page 134)
- Initial interview questions for victims, sample questions to help facilitators during their first meeting with victims (pages 135-136)
- Referral form containing information on the nature of the offense and contact information for the offender, his or her parents, and the victim (page 137)
- Report for court-based conference, informing the courts about the outcome of the conference (page 138)
- Report for school-based conference, informing school administration about the outcome of the conference (page 139)
- Facilitators' timeline, recommended time frames for receiving a case, arranging the conference, holding the conference, sending thank-you letters, collecting participant evaluation surveys and reporting back to the referral source (page 140)
- Information on conferencing "victimless" crimes and how to adapt the conference script (pages 141-143)
- Information on conferencing truancy and how truancy conferences differ from other conferences (page 144)
- Letter to parents for truancy conferencing, providing a description of the conferencing process and information on how to contact the Piedmont Dispute Resolution Center to schedule a conference (page 145)

Woodbury Police. In May 1995, Woodbury, Minnesota, became one of the first police departments in the nation to implement conferencing with juvenile offenders.

Materials include:

- Agreement form (page 146)
- Notice to parents of offenders about how the case will bc addressed (page 147)
- Conference participant pamphlet containing information about the program (pages 148-149)
- Participant questionnaire to rate their satisfaction with the process (page 150)
- Conference summary form to be completed after the conference (page 151)
- Letter to conference participants containing information about the program (page 152)

Peer Conferencing Program. These materials are from a peer conferencing program at a middle school in Pennsylvania. (The program is no longer operational.) Students were trained to run Real Justice conferences. Pairs of students, under the supervision of a faculty member, organized and facilitated conferences for incidents of wrongdoing.

Materials include:

- Case flow chart, outlining the procedures leading to a conference (page 153)
- Conference preparation guidelines for speaking with offenders, victims and supporters (pages 154-156)
- Conference preparation procedures, guidelines for the facilitators to keep in mind when running conferences (page 157)

Chapter 6: Restorative Practices — Beyond the Formal Conference

The following chapter is an adaptation of a paper that was presented by Ted Wachtel at the "Reshaping Australian Institutions Conference: Restorative Justice and Civil Society," Australian National University, Canberra, February 16-18, 1999.

Punitive Versus Permissive

Punishment in response to crime and other wrongdoing is the prevailing practice, not just in criminal justice systems but throughout most modern societies. Punishment is usually seen as the most appropriate response to crime and to wrongdoing in schools, families and workplaces. Those who fail to punish naughty children and offending youths and adults are often labelled as "permissive."

Figure 6: Punitive-Permissive Continuum

This punitive-permissive continuum (Figure 6) reflects the current popular view, but offers a very confined perspective and limited choice—to punish or not to punish. The only variable is the severity of the punishment, such as the amount of the fine or the length of the sentence. A more useful view of social control can be constructed by looking at the interplay of two more comprehensive variables, control and support.

Social Control Window

"Control" is defined as discipline or limit-setting and "support" as encouragement or nurturing. Now a high or low level of control can be combined with a high or low level of support to identify four general approaches

Punishment in response to crime and other wrongdoing is the prevailing practice, not just in criminal justice systems but throughout most modern societies.

to social control: neglectful, permissive, punitive (or retributive) and restorative (adapted by P. McCold & T. Wachtel from Glaser, 1969).

The traditional punitive-permissive continuum is subsumed within this more inclusive framework. The permissive approach (lower right of Figure 7) is comprised of low control and high support, a scarcity of limit-setting and an abundance of nurturing. Opposite permissive (upper left of Figure 7) is the punitive (or retributive) approach, high on control and low on support. Sadly, schools and courts in the United States and other countries have increasingly embraced the punitive approach, suspending and expelling more students and imprisoning more citizens than ever before. The third approach, when there is an absence of both limit-setting and nurturing, is neglectful (lower left of Figure 7).

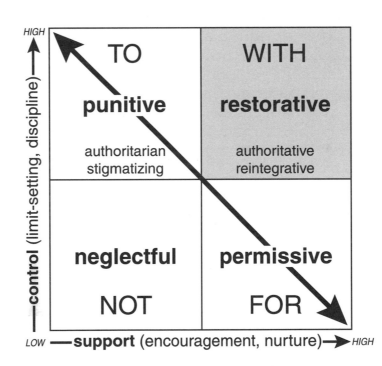

Figure 7: Social Control Window

The restorative approach confronts and disapproves of wrongdoing while supporting and valuing the intrinsic worth of the wrongdoer.

The fourth possibility is restorative (upper right of Figure 7), the approach to social control exemplified by Real Justice conferencing. Employing both high control and high support, the restorative approach confronts and disapproves of wrongdoing while supporting and valuing the intrinsic worth of the wrongdoer.

"Control" suggests high control of wrongdoing, not control of human beings in general. The ultimate goal is freedom from the kind of control that wrongdoers impose on others.

This Social Control Window can represent parenting styles. For example, there are neglectful parents who are absent, or abusive and permissive parents who are ineffectual or enabling. The term "authoritarian" has been used to describe the punitive parent while the restorative parent has been called "authoritative" (Baumrind, 1989). Further, one can apply John Braithwaite's (1989) terms to the window: "stigmatizing" responses to wrongdoing are punitive while "reintegrative" responses are restorative.

A few key words—NOT, FOR, TO and WITH—were initially introduced to help clarify the implications of the Social Control Window for the staff at the Community Service Foundation's schools and group homes. (Ted Wachtel, one of the authors of this handbook, is executive director of Community Service Foundation.) If the staff were neglectful toward the troubled youth in the agency's programs, they would NOT do anything in response to inappropriate behavior. If permissive, they would do everything FOR the young people in the programs, but ask little in return. If punitive, the staff would respond only by doing things TO the youth. But responding in a restorative manner, they do things WITH the young people when they are inappropriate and involve them directly in the process. A critical element of the restorative approach is that, whenever possible, WITH also includes victims, family, friends and community—those who been affected by the offender's behavior.

The implementation of restorative justice to date has been narrowly restricted.

Limitations of Formal Rituals

Although the restorative approach to social control expands the options beyond the traditional punitive-permissive continuum, the implementation of restorative justice to date has been narrowly restricted. Restorative justice is usually conceptualized in the form of community service projects designed to reintegrate offenders or formal rituals such as victim-offender mediation, sentencing circles and family group or community accountability conferences.

John Braithwaite, in his keynote address at the first North American Conference on Conferencing, asserted that "restorative justice will never become a mainstream alternative to retributive justice unless long-term R[esearch] and D[evelopment] programs show that it does have the capacity to reduce crime" (Braithwaite, 1998). If so, restorative justice as presently practiced is doomed to a peripheral role at the fringes of criminal justice and school disciplinary systems. There is all sorts of evidence that victims, offenders and their respective supporters find restorative justice rituals satisfying and just, but no one has yet conclusively demonstrated that restorative justice rituals significantly reduce re-offense rates or otherwise prevent crime.

Perhaps it is naive to think that a single restorative intervention can change the behavior and mindset of delinquent and high-risk youths, such as those who participate in Community Service Foundation (CSF) counseling, educational and residential programs. Yet young people who attend CSF programs do demonstrate significant positive behavior change. This is because, as Terry O'Connell remarked when he first visited one of the CSF schools in 1995, "You are running a conference all day long." Although the Foundation's staff never used the term "restorative justice" to describe its programs, there is now a growing realization that the Foundation's programs are characterized by the everyday use of a wide range of informal and formal restorative practices.

Restorative Practices Continuum

The term "restorative practice" includes any response to wrongdoing which falls within the parameters defined by the Social Control Window as both supportive and limit-setting. After examination, the possibilities become virtually unlimited. To illustrate, one can cite examples from everyday life in CSF's schools and group homes and place those along the restorative practices continuum. (See Figure 8 below.)

> *"Restorative justice will never become a mainstream alternative to retributive justice unless long-term R(esearch) and D(evelopment) programs show that it does have the capacity to reduce crime"*
> —Braithwaite, 1998

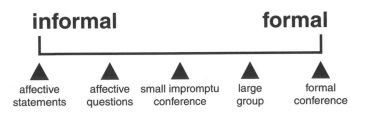

Figure 8: Restorative Practices Continuum

Moving from the left end of the continuum to the right, the restorative interventions become increasingly formal, involve more people, more planning, more time, are more complete in dealing with the offense, more structured, and due to all of those factors, may have more impact on the offender.

On the far left of the continuum is a simple affective response in which the wronged person lets the offender know how he or she feels about the incident. For example, one of the CSF staff might say, "Jason, you really hurt my feelings when you act like that. And it surprises me, because I don't think you want to hurt anyone on purpose." And that's all that is said. If a similar behavior happens again, the staff person might repeat the response or try a different restorative intervention, perhaps asking, "How do you think Mark felt when you did that?" and then waiting patiently for an answer.

In the middle of the continuum is the small impromptu conference, such as that facilitated by the CSF residential program director, while awaiting a court hearing about placing a 14-year-old boy in a CSF group home. His grandmother told the program director how on Christmas eve, several days before, the boy had gone over to a cousin's house without permission and without letting her know. He did not come back until the next morning, just barely in time for them to catch a bus to her sister's house for Christmas dinner. The program director got the grandmother talking about how that incident had affected her and how worried she was about her grandson. The boy was surprised by how deeply his behavior had affected his grandmother. He readily apologized.

Close to the far right of the continuum is a larger, more formal group process, still short of the formal conference. Two boys got into a fistfight, an unusual event at the CSF schools. After the fight was stopped, their parents were called to come and pick them up. If the boys wanted to return to the school, each boy had to phone and ask for an opportunity to convince the staff and his fellow students that he should be allowed back. Both boys called and came to school. One refused to take responsibility and had a defiant attitude. He was not re-admitted. The other was humble, even tearful. He listened attentively while staff and students told him how he had affected them, willingly took responsibility for his behavior, and got a lot of compliments about how he

One can create informal restorative interventions simply by asking offenders questions from the scripted formal conference.

handled the meeting. He was re-admitted and no further action was taken. The other boy was put in the juvenile detention center by his probation officer. Ideally, the probation officer would arrange for a formal family group conference under the auspices of the court, to address the probation violation, although that is not a normal practice at this time.

One can create informal restorative interventions simply by asking offenders questions from the scripted formal conference. "What happened?" "What were you thinking about at the time?" "Who do you think has been affected?" "How have they been affected?" Whenever possible, one provides those who have been affected with an opportunity to express their feelings to the offenders. The cumulative result of all of this affective exchange in a school is far more productive than lecturing, scolding, threatening or handing out detentions, suspensions and expulsions. The CSF teachers claim that classroom decorum in the CSF schools for troubled youth is better than in the local public schools. But interestingly, CSF staff rarely hold formal conferences. They have found that the more they rely on informal restorative practices in everyday life, the less they need formal restorative rituals.

In the Workplace

Restorative justice is a philosophy, not a model, and ought to guide the way one acts in all of one's dealings. In that spirit, an organization should use restorative practices with staff issues. The leadership should strive for an atmosphere where problems with staff are addressed in a restorative way, where staff can comfortably express concerns and criticisms of the leadership and where leaders are willing to admit and take responsibility for their own mistakes.

Last year several CSF employees became engaged in a squabble that was disrupting the workplace. The director felt removed enough from the situation to act as facilitator in a conference to deal with the spiraling conflict. In this conference there was no clearly identified wrongdoer. Rather, when invited to the conference, participants were each asked to take as much responsibility as possible for their part in the problem and were assured that everyone else was being asked to do the

Restorative justice is a philosophy, not a model, and ought to guide the way one acts in all of one's dealings.

same. There was a lot of self-disclosure and honesty in the preliminary discussions with each participant. The conference itself exceeded anyone's expectations. Not only did a great deal of healing taking place during the conference, but several individuals made plans to get together one-to-one to further resolve their differences. The conflict became ancient history and was no longer a factor in the CSF workplace.

At Home

Restorative practices are contagious, spreading from workplace to home. A woman related how she, her husband and her younger son restoratively confronted her young adult son, who had just entered the world of work. They told him how annoyed they were with his failure to get himself up on time in the morning. The parents expressed their embarrassment that their son had been late to work at a company where they knew a lot of his co-workers. They insisted that they were stepping back. If their son lost his job, it was not their problem, but his. As a result of the informal family group conference, the young man now sets three alarm clocks and gets to work on time.

A police officer who was trained in conferencing shared how he confronted his little boy, who had torn off a piece of new wallpaper, with questions from the conference. The youngster became very remorseful and acknowledged that he had hurt his mother, who loved the new wallpaper, and the workman he had watched put up the new wallpaper. The father felt satisfied that the intervention was far more effective than an old-fashioned scolding or punishment.

Varied Restorative Interventions

A police officer ran a variation on a family group conference with a dispute between neighbors about a barking dog; another held an impromptu conference on the front porch between a homeowner and an adolescent prankster who stole a lawn ornament. Still another police officer held a conference for the families of two runaways, helping the teenagers' understanding of how hurtful their actions were, although they had not committed a criminal offense that would typically require the officer's involvement. An assistant principal made

Restorative practices are contagious, spreading from workplace to home.

Beyond the formal criminal justice ritual, there are an infinite number of opportunities for restorative interventions.

two teenagers, on the verge of a fight, tell each other how they were feeling and brought them to quick resolution. A corrections officer addressed an inmate's angry outburst with a conference. A social worker got family members talking to each other in a real way about a teenager's persistent truancy and got the youth to start going to school. Beyond the formal criminal justice ritual, there are an infinite number of opportunities for restorative interventions.

Basics of Restorative Practice

For restorative practices to be effective in changing offender behavior, one should try to do the following:

1. *Foster awareness.* In the most basic intervention simply ask a few questions of the offender which foster awareness of how others have been affected by the wrongdoing. Or express one's own feelings to the offender. In more elaborate interventions one can provide an opportunity for others to express their feelings to the offenders.

2. *Avoid scolding or lecturing.* When offenders are exposed to other people's feelings and discover how victims and others have been affected by their behavior, they feel empathy for others. When scolded or lectured, they react defensively. They see themselves as victims and are distracted from noticing other people's feelings.

In a punitive intervention, offenders are completely passive. They just sit quietly and act like victims.

3. *Involve offenders actively.* All too often authorities try to hold offenders accountable by simply doling out punishment. But in a punitive intervention, offenders are completely passive. They just sit quietly and act like victims. In a restorative intervention, offenders are usually asked to speak. They face and listen to victims and others whom they have affected. They help decide how to repair the harm and must then keep their commitments. Offenders have an active role in a restorative process and are truly held accountable.

4. *Accept ambiguity.* Sometimes, as in a fight between two people, fault is unclear. In those cases one may have to accept ambiguity. Privately, before the conference, encourage individuals to take as much responsibility as possible for their part in the conflict. Even when offenders do not fully accept responsibility, victims often want to proceed. As long as everyone is fully informed of the ambiguous situation in advance, the

decision to proceed with a restorative intervention belongs to the participants.

5. *Separate the deed from the doer.* In an informal intervention, either privately with the offenders or publicly after the victims are feeling some resolution, express the assumption that the offenders did not mean to harm anyone or express surprise that the offenders would do something like that. When appropriate, one may want to cite some of their virtues or accomplishments. The goal is to recognize the offenders' worth and disapprove only of their wrongdoing.

6. *See every instance of wrongdoing and conflict as an opportunity for learning.* The teacher in the classroom, the police officer in the community, the probation officer with his caseload, and the corrections officer in the prison all have opportunities to model and teach. They can turn negative incidents into constructive events—building empathy and a sense of community that reduce the likelihood of negative incidents in the future.

The value of restorative practices in addressing crime and wrongdoing is not based on theory or wishful thinking, but on the results at CSF schools and group homes. Juvenile courts and schools from four counties send CSF 250 of their more troublesome young people at any one time. Thanks to restorative practices, these youth change their behaviors, cooperate, take positive leadership roles and confront each other about inappropriate behavior.

The CSF staff lacked an adequate way of expressing why these changes occurred until encountering the concept of restorative justice. CSF has undertaken a research project to evaluate more specifically how the agency's use of restorative practices impacts young people, what specifically changes, and to what extent those changes are sustained after students and clients leave CSF. But even without the study completed, it is obvious that something positive is happening as a result of systematic implementation of restorative practices in what might otherwise be a very negative and challenging environment.

The Community Service Foundation is the sponsoring agency for the Real Justice program and has subsidized its efforts since 1995. As Real Justice progressed in its efforts, training thousands in conference facilitation skills, it became apparent that many trainees never

The teacher in the classroom, the police officer in the community, the probation officer with his caseload, and the corrections officer in the prison all have opportunities to model and teach.

Real Justice developed the SaferSanerSchools™ program to help educators implement a range of restorative practices in schools.

conducted a conference. Some hesitated to facilitate a formal conference because they were afraid. Others did not have the authority to bypass existing procedures and sanctions, such as zero tolerance policies in schools. Nonetheless a large number of people have implemented restorative practices, using elements of the conference process informally as discussed above.

So Real Justice added the concept of restorative practices to its trainings, specifically encouraging people to try less formal interventions when they cannot do conferences. The idea has been well received, particularly among educators. While many teachers and administrators claimed that they did not have time or the right circumstance to pull together a full-blown conference, they were enthusiastic about more spontaneous restorative strategies. As a result of this positive response, Real Justice developed the SaferSanerSchools™ program to help educators implement a range of restorative practices in schools.

Police officers, probation officers, correctional officers and others have also faced obstacles in implementing conferencing. They may choose to proceed by using informal practices as a way to start making their own institutions and systems more restorative.

References

Baumrind, D. (1989). Presentation of an ongoing study at the 1989 American Psychological Association annual meeting, New Orleans, La., as reported by B. Bower, "Teenagers reap broad benefits from 'authoritative' parents." *Science News*, Vol.136, August 19, 1989.

Braithwaite, J. (1989). *Crime, Shame and Reintegration.* New York: Cambridge University Press.

Braithwaite, J. (1998). "Linking Crime Prevention to Restorative Justice." Presented at the First North American Conference on Conferencing, Minneapolis, Minn., August 6-8, 1998.

Glaser, D. (1969). *The Effectiveness of a Prison and Parole System.* Indianapolis, Ind.: Bobbs-Merrill, pp.289-297.

McCold, P. & Wachtel, B. (1998). *Restorative Policing Experiment: The Bethlehem Pennsylvania Police Family Group Conferencing Project.* A report to the National Institute of Justice, U.S. Department of Justice, Washington, D.C.

Moore, D.B. & Forsythe, L. (1995). *A New Approach to Juvenile Justice: An Evaluation of Family Conferencing in Wagga Wagga.* A report to the Criminology Research Council. Wagga Wagga, Australia: Centre for Rural Social Research, Charles Sturt University-Riverina.

Nathanson, D. (1992). *Shame and Pride: Affect, Sex and the Birth of the Self.* New York: Norton & Company.

Umbreit, M. & Fercello, C. (1998). "Family Group Conferencing Program Results in Client Satisfaction." *Juvenile Justice Update*, December/ January 1998, pp.3-4, 12-13.

Umbreit, M. & Fercello, C. (1999). *Client Evaluation of Family Group Conferencing in 12 Sites in 1st Judicial District of Minnesota.* Center for Restorative Justice and Mediation, School of Social Work, University of Minnesota.

Zehr, H. (1990). *Changing Lenses: A New Focus for Crime and Justice.* Scottdale, Pa.: Herald Press.

Appendix I
Conference Observation and Data Sheets

Conference Observation Sheet

The conference observation sheet (see pages 93-94) was originally developed for a study of police-run conferences in Bethlehem, Pennsylvania, to enhance the consistency in evaluations of conference facilitator performance (McCold & Wachtel, 1998). The form gives observers a structured framework for observing conferences, allowing for concrete feedback to facilitators.

In the first part of the conference observation sheet, observers write their name, the name of the facilitator, case-identifying information, the nature of the offense, the date of the conference, the times when the conference begins and ends, and the time when participants have finished socializing after the conference ("Soc. Time").

The second part is a checklist of seven items that facilitators should do before beginning every conference. These include:

1) Introducing all participants
2) Obtaining permission for observers
3) Acknowledging appreciation of everyone's effort to attend
4) Setting the conference focus
5) Telling offenders they have the right to terminate the conference at any time
6) Checking that offenders understand this right
7) Making sure offenders take clear responsibility for their behavior as they tell their story in the conference

On the third part of the conference observation sheet, observers make a check each time they observe the facilitator doing any of nine types of actions, both inappropriate and appropriate, during the conference. These are:

1) Use of silence (appropriate)
2) Refocus discussion (appropriate)
3) Failure to refocus (inappropriate)
4) Interrupt participant (inappropriate)
5) Redundant question (inappropriate)
6) Avoidance of emotion (inappropriate)
7) Restating comments (inappropriate)
8) Nodding head (inappropriate)
9) Adding language (inappropriate)

For the bottom section of the first page, observers watch the conference and simply make a check each time a participant—offender, victim, victim supporter, offender supporter or facilitator—exhibits a particular behavior. The diagonal lines allow for observation of up to two of each type of participant. Observers can make further divisions if there are, for example, three victims or four offender supporters.

Some of the items are applicable only to particular participants. The items are:

1) showing respect for the offender
2) showing respect for the victim
3) expressing disapproval of the act
4) expressing disapproval of the offender
5) apologizing
6) forgiving the offender
7) being defiant
8) describing the consequences of the act
9) suggesting reparation to the victim
10) suggesting reparation to the community

The second page of the form includes a list of questions about the facilitator, victim, offender and other participants which are completed after the conference. These are rated on a five-point scale, ranging from "not at all" to "completely." The items are:

About facilitator
1) Did the facilitator maintain the distinction between the person and behavior?
2) Was any reparation suggested by the facilitator?
3) Was the reparation outcome affected by the facilitator?
4) Did the facilitator lecture the offender?
5) To what extent did the facilitator adhere to conference facilitation protocol?

About victim
1) Did the victim seem satisfied with the outcome?
2) Did the victim indicate a sense of forgiveness?

About offender
1) Did the offender appear to understand the injury caused to the victim?
2) Did the offender seem to express sincere remorse?
3) Did the offender appear to end with a feeling of pride?

About other participants
1) Did the offender's family volunteer future responsibility for the offender?
2) Did the offender's supporters volunteer future responsibility for the offender?

3) Was there a strong sense of reconciliation (reintegration)?

The last section of the form includes questions about which participant seemed most punitive, if there was a restitution agreement, whether action was proposed to prevent future similar injuries, and whether a follow-up plan was agreed to in the conference. Observers should also describe any other deviations from standard conference facilitation protocol.

Conference Data Sheet

The Conference Data Sheet (page 95) is for facilitators to record basic case information, general outcomes, and to evaluate their own experience after the conference.

Participant Data Sheet

The Participant Data Sheet (page 96) is used to record details about the offenders, victims and all other conference participants.

CONFERENCE OBSERVATION SHEET

Observer:_____ Case Identifier:_____

Facilitator:_____ Offense:_____

Date:_____ conference time begin:_____ a.m. p.m. conference time end:_____ a.m. p.m. social time end:_____ a.m. p.m.

☐ Introductions

☐ Permission for observers

☐ Appreciation of effort

☐ Set conference focus

☐ Offender right to terminate

☐ Check for understanding

☐ Stay with offender appropriately

use of silence	
refocus discussion	
failure to refocus	
interrupt participant	
redundant question	
avoidance of emotion	
restating comments	
nodding head	
adding language	

	Offender	Victim	Victim supporters	Arresting officer	Offender supporters	*Facilitator*
respect for offender						
respect for victim						
disapproval of act						
disapproval of offender						
apologizes						
offender is forgiven						
is defiant						
consequences of act						
suggest reparation to victim						
suggest reparation to community						

FACILITATOR

Did the facilitator maintain the distinction between person and behavior?
□ not at all　□ a little　□ somewhat　□ mostly　□ completely

Was any reparation suggested by the facilitator?
□ not at all　□ a little　□ somewhat　□ mostly　□ completely

Was the reparation outcome affected by the facilitator?
□ not at all　□ a little　□ somewhat　□ mostly　□ completely

Did the facilitator lecture the offender?
□ not at all　□ a little　□ somewhat　□ mostly　□ completely

To what extent did the facilitator adhere to conference facilitation protocol?
□ not at all　□ a little　□ somewhat　□ mostly　□ completely

VICTIM

Did the victim seem satisfied with the outcome?
□ not at all　□ a little　□ somewhat　□ mostly　□ completely

Did the victim indicate a sense of forgiveness?
□ not at all　□ a little　□ somewhat　□ mostly　□ completely

OFFENDER

Did the offender appear to understand the injury caused to the victim?
□ not at all　□ a little　□ somewhat　□ mostly　□ completely

Did the offender seem to express sincere remorse?
□ not at all　□ a little　□ somewhat　□ mostly　□ completely

Did the offender appear to end with a feeling of pride?
□ not at all　□ a little　□ somewhat　□ mostly　□ completely

OTHER PARTICIPANTS

Did the offender's family volunteer future responsibility for the offender?
□ not at all　□ a little　□ somewhat　□ mostly　□ completely

Did the offender's other supporters volunteer future responsibility for the offender?
□ not at all　□ a little　□ somewhat　□ mostly　□ completely

Was there a strong sense of reconciliation (reintegration)?
□ not at all　□ a little　□ somewhat　□ mostly　□ completely

Which participant seemed most punitive? _____

Was restitution from the offender agreed to?

no □　yes
　□ money　*amount total $* _____　*amount monthly $* _____
　□ personal service　*total hours* _____
　□ community service　*total hours* _____
　□ other: specify _____

Was action proposed to prevent future similar injuries?
□ no　□ yes: *describe* _____

Was a follow-up plan agreed to?
□ no　□ yes: *describe* _____

Other deviations from protocol _____

CONFERENCE DATA SHEET

Date of conference: ___/___/___   Date of offense: ___/___/___

Conference location: _____

Name of facilitator: _____

Referral source: ☐ Police   Conference type: ☐ Police diversion
                 ☐ Probation   ☐ Pre-disposition
                 ☐ Judicial   ☐ Post-disposition
                 ☐ Other: specify_____   ☐ Other: specify_____

Description of offense: _____

_____

_____

Name of primary offender (or case number): _____

Were the victim(s) and offender(s) acquainted before the offense?
    ☐ yes   ☐ no
    IF YES: How were they known to each other?
    ☐ friend   ☐ acquaintance   ☐ neighbor   ☐ other: specify _____

Who was present at the conference?

        number of offenders:_____   number of victims: _____
    number of offender supporters:_____   number of victim supporters: _____
            total number of participants (excluding yourself):_____

Was a formal agreement signed?   ☐ yes   ☐ no   (IF YES, attach a copy)

Was a formal apology offered?   ☐ yes   ☐ no

How would you rate this conference process?
    ☐ very positive   ☐ positive   ☐ mixed   ☐ negative   ☐ very negative

How would you rate this conference outcome?
    ☐ very positive   ☐ positive   ☐ mixed   ☐ negative   ☐ very negative

Would you say the tone of the conference was generally

    ☐ friendly   ☐ hostile   ☐ other: specify:_____

How long did this conference take? (hours : minutes) _____ : _____

Not counting the time of the conference itself, how much time
did you spend preparing for the conference? (hours : minutes) _____ : _____

How would you rate your experience from 1 (horrible) to 10 (ecstatic)? _____

ADDITIONAL COMMENTS:
    (e.g., offender parents difficult, victim found healing, offender refused responsibility, etc.)

PARTICIPANT DATA SHEET

Age of offender #___ :_____

☐ male ☐ female

☐ white ☐ black ☐ Hispanic

☐ other (specify):_____

Age of offender #___ :_____

☐ male ☐ female

☐ white ☐ black ☐ Hispanic

☐ other (specify):_____

Age of offender #___ :_____

☐ male ☐ female

☐ white ☐ black ☐ Hispanic

☐ other (specify):_____

Check all offender supporters present:

Offender #_____

☐ both parents

☐ mother only

☐ father only

☐ siblings (number:_____)

☐ other relative (specify): _____

☐ other relative (specify): _____

☐ other non-relative (specify):_____

☐ other non-relative (specify):_____

Offender #_____

☐ both parents

☐ mother only

☐ father only

☐ siblings (number:_____)

☐ other relative (specify): _____

☐ other relative (specify): _____

☐ other non-relative (specify):_____

☐ other non-relative (specify):_____

Offender #_____

☐ both parents

☐ mother only

☐ father only

☐ siblings (number:_____)

☐ other relative (specify): _____

☐ other relative (specify): _____

☐ other non-relative (specify):_____

☐ other non-relative (specify):_____

Age of victim #___ :_____

☐ male ☐ female

☐ white ☐ black ☐ Hispanic

☐ other (specify):_____

Age of victim #___ :_____

☐ male ☐ female

☐ white ☐ black ☐ Hispanic

☐ other (specify):_____

Age of victim #___ :_____

☐ male ☐ female

☐ white ☐ black ☐ Hispanic

☐ other (specify):_____

Check all victim supporters present:

Victim # _____

☐ both parents

☐ mother only

☐ father only

☐ siblings (number:_____)

☐ other relative (specify): _____

☐ other relative (specify): _____

☐ other non-relative (specify):_____

☐ other non-relative (specify):_____

Victim # _____

☐ both parents

☐ mother only

☐ father only

☐ siblings (number:_____)

☐ other relative (specify): _____

☐ other relative (specify): _____

☐ other non-relative (specify):_____

☐ other non-relative (specify):_____

Victim # _____

☐ both parents

☐ mother only

☐ father only

☐ siblings (number:_____)

☐ other relative (specify): _____

☐ other relative (specify): _____

☐ other non-relative (specify):_____

☐ other non-relative (specify):_____

USE ADDITIONAL FORMS IF NECESSARY. REPRODUCE AND ATTACH.

Appendix II
Conferencing Program
Literature Samples

REF......................./..............

WAGGA WAGGA POLICE PATROL
JUVENILE CAUTIONING CONFERENCE AGREEMENT

DATE: ..../.........../..............

NAME: ....

ADDRESS: ....

....

My family and I will complete the following undertaking/s, which have been agreed to at this Cautioning Conferencing today.

1. A personal apology to the victim	YES/NO	VICTIM TO ACKNOWLEDGE WHEN UNDERTAKINGS ARE COMPLETED
A written apology to the victim	YES/NO	

VICTIM: ....

....

....

2. Compensation/Reparation   YES/NO

....

....

....

VICTIM TO ACKNOWLEDGE WHEN UNDERTAKINGS ARE COMPLETED

....

Date: ..../.........../..............

Please return to:
Cautioning Sergeant
Police Station
WAGGA WAGGA 2650.

3. OTHER MATTERS:
P.C.Y.C. Program   YES/NO

....

....

I agree to the above: .... (young person)

witnessed and agreed: .... (parent/guardian)

witnessed: .... (police officer)

Dated at Wagga Wagga ..../.............../.......................

Family Group Conferencing

Working Together to Heal the Harm

Central Bucks School District

"Anyone can become angry—that is easy. But to be angry with the right person, to the right degree, at the right time, for the right purpose, and in the right way — this is not easy."

— Aristotle, *The Nicomacean Ethics*

∿ ∿ ∿

In the Central Bucks School District we work hard to maintain a safe, caring school community where every child can feel the safety and security necessary for learning and personal growth to flourish.

Any form of harming behavior such as verbal or physical assault, bullying, stealing, harassment, or vandalism erodes this important sense of safety and community, and diminishes the overall learning atmosphere.

One innovative way in which the Central Bucks School District has been responding pro-actively to harming behavior is through a technique known as FAMILY GROUP CONFERENCING.

IF YOU HAVE ANY QUESTIONS concerning Family Group Conferencing, please contact the Guidance Office in your school.

Central Bucks School District
16 Welden Drive
Doylestown, PA 18901

What is Family Group Conferencing?

Whenever a harming incident occurs in school, such as verbal or physical assault, bullying, stealing, sexual harassment or vandalism, the resulting negative impacts can be felt by many.

Often those responsible for the harming incident did not intend or anticipate the full extent of the resulting harm. The degree of impact varies, but the person or persons harmed, the person or persons responsible for the harming, family members, school staff, friends, and classmates are often left feeling hurt, angry, fearful, confused, remorseful or helpless in being able to effectively respond to the specific harm which has been done.

The Family Group Conference provides a safe, structured forum where those persons most affected by the harming event are able to sit down together, and honestly and effectively address the impact of the incident. The conference is coordinated by a Central Bucks School District staff member trained in the procedure. The coordinator moves the group through a scripted, supportive process which empowers all participants to:

(1) Safely express their feelings and concerns

(2) Explore the extent and variety of ways people have been affected by the harming behavior

(3) Engage everyone in developing a meaningful signed "Agreement" which lists specific ways to begin the process of "healing the harm"

What are the goals of this process?

The Family Group Conference only focuses on one specific incident of harming behavior. It does not seek to fix blame, or determine who is "good" or 'bad" but affirms the integrity and respect of all the participants. Its goals include:

- To provide a safe opportunity to express genuine feelings, concerns, hurts and apologies

- To increase awareness and understanding of the full impact of the harming behavior

- To enhance the dignity and respect of all participants

- To empower everyone involved with the opportunity to play a significant role in "healing the harm"

- To develop an "agreement" to which all participants can sign and commit

- To affirm a strong sense of safety and care to the school community

- To provide a powerful learning experience

- To support "positive closure"

Who is involved?

It is important to note that the Family Group Conference procedure is strictly voluntary, and no one is pressured to participate. Typically, a conference lasts no more then one hour, and the participants include:

- The person or persons harmed

- The person or persons who are responsible for the harm and who willingly acknowledge responsibility for the incident

- Other persons who have been impacted by the harming in some way and are willing to support the procedure

Who benefits?

Numerous Family Group Conferences have been conducted in the Central Bucks School District. Participant satisfaction has consistently been very encouraging. Although there is nothing magical about a conference, participants report that they feel empowered and supported in bringing positive closure to difficult incidents of harm, and that a sense of safety and care was reaffirmed to the school community.

COMMUNITY CONFERENCE REPARATIVE AGREEMENT

Name:_____ Offense:_____

Date:_____ Conference Site: _____

Coordinator : _____ Facilitators:_____

In accordance with the purpose of the program, the agreement *must* demonstrate how the offender will (1) restore the victim if there is a direct victim and (2) make amends to the community. The agreement *may* include limited assessment, competency-building, and/or skill-building of the offender (an initial or introductory commitment only).

Required - Restore the victim if there is a direct victim:

_____

_____

_____

_____

_____

Supervised by (Liaison or Lead Facilitator):_____

Required - Make amends to the community:

_____

_____

_____

_____

_____

_____

_____

Supervised by (Liaison or Lead Facilitator):_____

Optional - Limited assessment, competency-building, and/or skill-building of the offender (an initial or introductory commitment only):

_____

_____

_____

_____

_____

Supervised by (Liaison or Lead Facilitator):_____

Agreement Deadline:_____

I, _____, have participated in developing this contract and agree to complete all conditions by the deadline of _____. I understand all aspects of this contract as presented to me. It is my responsibility to complete the conditions outlined in this contract. I understand that the program will monitor and verify my compliance with these terms. I understand that if I do not complete my responsibilities outlined here, or if the deadline is missed, my case will be referred back to the court for further action.

_____ _____
(Offender Participant)   (Date)

Approved by (only first names or initials are required):

_____   _____

_____   _____

_____   _____

_____   _____

_____   _____
(Facilitator)   (Facilitator)

_____
(Coordinator)

Date completed:_____ Verified by:_____

Central City Neighborhoods Partnership

Community Conferencing

A Restorative Justice Program for Community Resolution of Crime

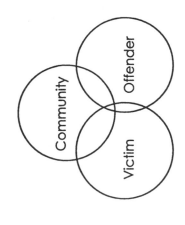

Community

Offender

Victim

110 E. 18th Street
Minneapolis, MN 55403
612/871-8100
Fax: 879-2917

◆ This program receives financial support from the Minnesota Department of Corrections, The Minneapolis Foundation, The McKnight Foundation, and the Minneapolis Police Department Law Enforcement Block Grant program.

Primary Partners

Minneapolis Office of the City Attorney
Minneapolis Police Department

Supporting Partners

Augustana Apartments
Basilica of St. Mary
Cathedral Church of St. Mark
Catholic Charities
Central Lutheran Church
Central Community Housing Trust
Centro Legal
Citizens Council
City of Lakes Transitional Care Center
Community Emergency Services
Elliot Park Community Center
Emerson School
First Covenant Church
First Unitarian Society
Hennepin County Department of Community Corrections
Hennepin County District Court
Hennepin United Methodist Church
La Oportunidad
Minnesota Coalition Against Prostitution
Minneapolis Center for Neighborhoods
Minneapolis Public Library
Neighborhood Planning for Community Revitalization
Oficina Legal
180 Degrees
Opportunity Partners
People Serving People
Plymouth Congregational Church
Red Eye Theater
Salvation Army
Sentencing to Service
Somali Community of Minnesota
Stevens Community Associates
Twin Cities AIDS Ride
United Way Volunteer Program
Urban League
Wesley United Methodist Church
Westminster Presbyterian Church

12/98

RESULTS?

So far, approximately 90% of offenders who attended a conference have fulfilled their contracts with the community and remain crime-free. Nearly 100% of community members report that they were satisfied with the outcome, and that they would recommend the program to others.

One participant says, "I feel this was an excellent process. The court would have given him a slap on the wrist or a meaningless fine. This all had meaning and connection to the incident."

Please call our office for an update on conferenced cases and outcomes.

BACKGROUND

The Central City Neighborhoods Partnership (CCNP) is engaged in a cooperative effort to identify systemic shortcomings in the criminal justice system and to develop an action plan for change. Residents of the Stevens Square, Elliot Park, Loring Park, and Downtown neighborhoods of Minneapolis have been exploring criminal justice issues together since the fall of 1994. Viewing the combination of low-level crime and recidivism as an ongoing threat to community livability, these citizens are engaging local institutions, both public and private, in the application of restorative justice principles to a proactive, innovative method of holding offenders accountable for their actions.

103

COMMUNITY CONFERENCING: CONFRONTING CRIME IN YOUR NEIGHBORHOOD

Community Conferencing is a neighborhood-based restorative justice program that holds offenders directly accountable to the community for crimes that affect quality of life. A pilot project of the Central City Neighborhoods Partnership (CCNP) in Minneapolis, the program combines face-to-face dialogue with creative restitution and/or community service to resolve crime at the community level in a constructive and meaningful way. In this manner, the community is addressing livability offenses such as theft, trespassing, consuming, public urination, shoplifting, graffiti, and soliciting prostitution.

Steps in a Conference

- Offender, victim, and supporters meet with community members in the neighborhood of the offense
- People take turns describing the impact of the behavior
- The group creates a reparative agreement, decided by consensus
- Offender makes amends to the victim and community

Community Conferencing serves as a court diversion for non-violent adult offenders who are willing to acknowledge their wrongdoing and make reparation to those they have harmed. In successful cases, the offender's charges are dismissed, with no plea on record.

WHAT IS RESTORATIVE JUSTICE?

Restorative justice is a way of addressing crime (or conflict) that focuses on repairing harm. The goal is not to penalize, but to restore. It makes victims central and empowers them to have a key role in the justice process.

- Victim has a voice
- Offender is accountable
- Community is involved
- Damage of crime is repaired
- Offender is reintegrated
- Individual needs are met
- Relationships are strengthened

Community Conferencing is just one of many restorative justice models.

Why Do We Need It?

The criminal justice system is jammed and its resources are scarce. Creating meaningful consequences for nuisance crimes is not a high priority. Moreover, victims are often left out of the picture — both individuals who are harmed and the community itself.

With restorative justice, crime can be an opportunity to make our community stronger, by holding offenders accountable and involving citizens in the process. The community can support victims, reinforce the standards of acceptable behavior, and create space for dialogue and healing.

Get Involved!

Community Conferencing is an initiative of the Stevens Square, Loring Park, Downtown, and Elliot Park neighborhood organizations. The program operates in a geographic area covering downtown Minneapolis and stretching from the river to Franklin Avenue, bordered by 35W on the east and I-94 on the west. Any person who lives, works, or worships in these neighborhoods can be involved.

➤ First call the program to tell us you are interested! (612/871-8100)

➤ **Participate in a conference** with other community members

➤ If interested, **become a conference facilitator** (free training available)

➤ Let us know about potential work projects in your neighborhood

➤ Become a "liaison" -- **assist a victim or offender** through the process

➤ Attend a monthly **advisory meeting** to help direct the program

➤ Be a **translator** at a conference

➤ Get on our **mailing list** for updates

➤ Make a **donation** to help the project

Community members make Community Conferencing happen. Community empowerment is what it's all about. Ordinary citizens are getting involved in the justice process to address concerns in their neighborhood. Volunteers facilitate conferences, and a citizen advisory board steers the program. This is a unique opportunity to have a direct role in tackling the crimes that affect you where you live and work.

Conference Evaluation: Third Party Participant

Name_____ _____

Date_____

Case #_____

Why did you choose to participate in the conference?

_____

_____

- Outcome

Do you feel the conference properly addressed the offense? (Yes/No)

Do you feel justice was served? (Yes/No)

Did you personally experience any benefits from participating in this conference?

(Yes/No)_____

_____

- Process

Was the offender treated fairly? (Yes/No)

Were you given ample opportunity to have input? (Yes/No)

Did the facilitator do a proper job in leading the conference? (Yes/No)

In your opinion, was the conference preferable to having this situation handled by the court system? (Yes/No)

Please add any comments and/or suggestions you may have:

_____

_____

_____

Central City Neighborhoods Partnership

Conference Evaluation: Facilitator

Your Name_____

Date_____

Case #_____

- Outcome

Did the conference properly address the offense, in your opinion? (Yes/No)

Did it appear to you that justice was served? (Yes/No) Comments:

_____

Do you feel more connected to the community as a result of your participation? (Yes/No)

Was there anything noteworthy about the conference?

_____

_____

- Process

Did the co-facilitator do a proper job in leading the conference? (Yes/No) Comments:

_____

Are there areas of improvement to be made?

_____

_____

- Overall

In your opinion, was the conference preferable to having this situation handled by the court system? (Yes/No)

Would you like to facilitate again? (Yes/No)

Would you be interested in a follow-up meeting with the offender? (Yes/No)

Please add any comments and/or suggestions you may have:

_____

_____

_____

Conference Evaluation: Program Participant

Your Name:_____

Date_____

Case #_____

- Outcome

Yes/No Did the conference properly address the offense?
Yes/No Were you satisfied with the outcome?
Yes/No Do you feel you were appropriately held accountable for the offense you committed?
Yes/No Do you feel justice was served?
Yes/No Are you more aware of the impact of your behavior on the community?
Yes/No Do you live within the general vicinity of the crime scene?
Yes/No Do you now feel more connected to this community?
Yes/No Are there things that you think the court system could have handled better in this situation? Please explain:_____

_____

- Process

Yes/No Do you feel your needs were met during the conference?
Yes/No Were you were treated fairly?
Yes/No Did the facilitator do a proper job in leading the conference?
Yes/No Did someone previously unknown to you come to support you at the conference?
Yes/No If so, was it helpful?

- Overall

Yes/No In your opinion, was the conference preferable to having this situation handled by the court system?
Yes/No How does the conference compare to what you expected to face in the court system?_____

_____

Yes/No Would you recommend conferencing to another person in a similar situation?

Please add any comments and/or suggestions you may have:

_____

_____

_____

Conference Evaluation: Program Participant

Nombre_____

Fecha_____

Numero de Caso_____

- Resultado

___Si ___No Era la conferencia apropriada a la ofensa criminal?
___Si ___No Estas satisfecho con el resultado?
___Si ___No Crees que la responsabilidad implicita era apropriada a la ofensa?
___Si ___No Crees que se ha hecho justicia?
___Si ___No Vives cerca del lugar donde cometiste el crimen?
___Si ___No Sientes ahora que formas mas parte integrante de la comunidad?
___Si ___No Hay cosas que el tribunal podria hacer major en esta situatcion? Explica por favor:

_____

_____

- El Procedimiento

___Si ___No Has recibido lo que necesita de la conferencia?
___Si ___No Fuiste tratado justamente?
___Si ___No Ha dirigido bien la conferencia el director?
___Si ___No Hay alguien, a quien no conoces, quien vino a la conferencia para darte su apoyo?
___Si ___No Fue provechoso su apoyo?

- De Conjunto

___Si ___No En tu opinion, fue preferible la conferencia al sistema tribunal?
Como comparas esta conferencia con la expectiva de que tienes del sistema judicial?

_____

_____

___Si ___No Recomendarias la conferencia a otras personas en situaciones semejantes?
Puedes anadir algunos comentarios que te parezcan convenientes:

_____

_____

Central City Neighborhoods Partnership

Conference Evaluation: Offender Supporter

Name_____

Date_____

Case #_____

What is your relationship to the offender?
___Family or personal friend ___Community Liaison ___Other:_____

- Outcome

Do you feel the conference properly addressed the offense? (Yes/No)

Do you feel justice was served? (Yes/No)

Did you personally experience any benefits from participating in this conference?
(Yes/No)_____

_____

- Process

Was the offender treated fairly? (Yes/No)

Were you given ample opportunity to have input? (Yes/No)

Did the facilitator do a proper job in leading the conference? (Yes/No)

In your opinion, was the conference preferable to having this situation handled by the court system? (Yes/No)

Please add any comments and/or suggestions you may have:

_____

_____

_____

Central City Neighborhoods Partnership

Conference Evaluation: Victim/Community Participant

Your Name_____

Date_____

Case #_____

- Outcome

Yes/No   Did the conference properly address the offense?
Yes/No   Were you satisfied with the outcome?
Yes/No   Do you feel justice was served?
Yes/No   After the conference, has your level of fear changed? Please explain:

_____

_____

Yes/No   Do you feel more connected to the community as an outcome of this process?
Yes/No   Are there things that you think the court system could have handled better in this situation? Please explain: _____

_____

- Process

Yes/No   Did you feel safe and secure from the offender during the conference?
Yes/No   Do you feel your needs were met during the conference?
Yes/No   Were you were treated fairly?
Yes/No   Did the facilitator do a proper job in leading the conference?
Yes/No   Did someone previously unknown to you come to support you at the conference?
Yes/No   If so, was it helpful?

- Overall

Yes/No   In your opinion, was the conference preferable to having this situation handled by the court system? Please explain: _____

_____

Yes/No   Would you be interested in a follow-up meeting with the offender?
Yes/No   Would you recommend conferencing to another person in a similar situation?
Yes/No   Would you be interested in participating again?
Yes/No   Do you know someone else who might like to be involved?
           Name:_____Number:_____

Please add any comments and/or suggestions you may have:

Central City Neighborhoods Partnership

Conference Evaluation: Victim Supporter

Your Name_____

Date_____

Case #_____

What is your relationship to the victim?

___Family or personal friend ___Community Liaison ___Other:_____

- Outcome

Do you feel the conference properly addressed the offense? (Yes/No)

Do you feel justice was served? (Yes/No)

Did you personally experience any benefits from participating in this conference?
(Yes/No)_____

_____

- Process

Was the victim treated fairly? (Yes/No)

Were you given ample opportunity to have input? (Yes/No)

Did the facilitator do a proper job in leading the conference? (Yes/No)

In your opinion, was the conference preferable to having this situation handled by the court system? (Yes/No)

Please add any comments and/or suggestions you may have:

_____

_____

_____

Community Conferencing Pre-Meeting Checklist ☐Victim Group ☐Offender Group

Facilitators:_____ Date:_____ (<u>Turn this in to CCNP when complete.</u>)

NOTE: Avoid using the word "offender" in conversation -- substitute their name or refer to "person arrested," "person responsible for this incident," "person who committed the crime."

Introductions
☐ First names only: who is here, and their relation to the offender, victim, or community.
☐ Explain that facilitators are staff/volunteers who do not work for the courts (n'hood program).

Purpose of Program
☐ The Community Conference is a meeting to resolve an incident with the people affected.
☐ This is a restorative justice program, which means that the focus is on repairing the harm.
☐ This is not about shaming or punishment; this is different from the traditional court process.
☐ The goals of this program are to give (the offender) a way to make amends, restore the victim, and strengthen the community.
☐ People who were involved or affected will sit in a circle with their supporters and the facilitators.
☐ The group will talk about the impact of the incident and how to repair the harm.

Background
☐ Brief description of incident. (Type of crime, date, location.)
☐ How the case got here: City Attorney's Office approved the case for Conferencing; offender agreed to participate in program rather than face prosecution: has agreed to take responsibility.
☐ If an agreement is reached and carried out, and if there is no new arrest for a "same or similar" offense in the next year, then charges are dropped and there is no conviction on record. If the conference doesn't happen or the agreement is not fulfilled, then the case is returned to court.
☐ *Offender:* <u>Are you ready to take full responsibility?</u> (It is a prerequisite for the program that you freely and fully admit to this offense.) Please describe what happened.

Participants
☐ The people who will be at this conference are:
☐ *Offender:* As you know, it is required that you bring a supporter with you. This is for your benefit, so that the discussion and the agreement will be balanced and fair. It is also a protection for the program -- a witness who participates with you and ensures fairness by signing the agreement.
☐ *Offender:* Who will you bring as a supporter? We are required to contact your supporter by mail or phone to give them information ahead of time. Full Name:_____
Phone Number or Address_____

Facilitators
☐ Facilitators are neutral. We are not judges, and we have no decision making power.
☐ Facilitators are trained to follow a script for the conference; we will not interject or give our opinion
☐ We are required by law to maintain confidentiality, although any of *you* can speak freely about the conference. If we learn about abuse of a child or vulnerable adult, then we must report it.

The Conference
☐ Each person will have a chance to speak, one at a time.
☐ First: Admission of responsibility. Person arrested takes ownership, tells what happened.
☐ Second: Discussion of impact. People describe how they have been affected.
☐ Third: Repairing the harm. The whole group works out an agreement that is acceptable to all.
☐ Closing: Final comments.
☐ Afterward: sign agreement, share refreshments, talk with one another (reintegration, closure).

The Agreement

- ❑ The agreement should be meaningful to the victim and community; the goal is to repair the harm.
- ❑ Making an agreement is *not the same as deciding a sentence;* the contract is not a punishment.
- ❑ According to the program guidelines, the agreement *must* demonstrate how the offender will (1) restore the victim if there is a direct victim and (2) make amends to the community. The agreement *may* include limited assessment, competency-building, and/or skill-building of the offender (as long as it is an initial or introductory commitment only) -- like a class, workshop, group, meeting, or assessment – but this part is not required for the agreement.
- ❑ Each person will be asked to give their input and help decide on the agreement.
- ❑ There are no court rules about what goes into the agreement.
- ❑ You set the deadline; the court prefers that the agreement be complete within 6 months.
- ❑ Each agreement is different, designed to fit the case by the people who are involved. Our emphasis is not on consistency. That is the court's job. *Customizing* is more important here.
- ❑ Agreement items need to be workable and specific: days, hours, deadlines, means of verification.
- ❑ Compensation to victim/community: here is a handout of some community service options in the area. You can use this as a resource, but this not a "menu" that you have to use.
- ❑ Be as flexible and creative as you want. Think about what would best repair the harm in this case. Ideas?_____
- ❑ You can put a follow-up meeting in the agreement if you want to; suggest this in the conference.
- ❑ Check out your ideas *before* the conference to get the details about when, where, and how they can be done. It would be a shame to miss an opportunity because we just need more info.

Discussion

- ❑ *Victims*: (Each person) How have you been affected?
- ❑ *Offender:* What is your current situation (working, in school, etc.)?_____
- ❑ *Offender:* Any limitations, physical or otherwise?_____
- ❑ *Supporters*: How has this affected you? What would you like to see the conference accomplish?

Ground rules

- ❑ There are ground rules for everyone in the conference: no disrespect, no interruptions, no insults. Be honest, be willing to tell your story, be willing to listen. Come willing to work out an agreement.
- ❑ Strong feelings are welcome. Call a time out if you want to talk privately with a facilitator. Breaks may be taken for bathrooms and water. Questions or concerns?

Miscellaneous

- ❑ The location of the conference will be.....(remind the group, provide directions if necessary).
- ❑ People from the community and court system want to learn how this works. Observers sit outside the circle and do not participate. Would it be okay with you to have 1-2 observers? Circle:YES/No
- ❑ This program is new, so we need your feedback. We will send you an evaluation in the mail with a stamped envelope. Please tell us your level of satisfaction. This is important for quality control.
- ❑ Offender: We have a cancellation policy. If the conference is cancelled within one week of the conference, the case will automatically be returned to court. Also, if anything happens at any time that would prevent you from attending on time, call the office *immediately* and leave your message, or the case may automatically be returned to court. The number is 871-8100.
- ❑ Facilitators: please have the Consent Form signed by offender and turn this in to CCNP.

Conclusion

- ❑ Any questions? You can call the program at 871-8100 if you want to talk to staff.
- ❑ Thanks for coming. We'll see you at the conference!   CCNP 2/99

CCNP RESTORATIVE JUSTICE REVIEW

Central City Neighborhoods Partnership

| Volume 1, Issue 1 | (612) 871-8100 | February-March 1999 |

Downtown Minneapolis Neighborhood Association
Stevens Square Community Organization
Citizens for a Loring Park Community
Elliot Park Neighborhood Inc.

Central City Neighborhoods Partnership
Restorative Justice Program

Community Leaders Hold First Quarterly Retreat

 On February 20th, the facilitators and Advisory Team members of the CCNP Restorative Justice Program gathered in Mound, MN at Our Lady of the Lake Church.

It was a lovely Saturday and the group spent some time getting to know one another better and then set about the business of the day.

Through role-plays, new facilitators got a chance to develop some of their skills needed in leading conferences. It was also a valuable opportunity for more experienced facilitators to keep current with the changes that have been implemented by the program over the past few months.

Later in the day, Sue Stacey, from the Minnesota Department of Corrections, helped the group brainstorm ideas for a formal mission statement for the CCNP Community Conferencing pilot program. Together we shared our ideas on what this program is about and came up with two possible mission statements. They will be forwarded to the CCNP Restorative Justice Policy Committee for consideration. Anybody involved with the program is welcome to attend the next Policy Committee meeting on March 29th to have a voice in this process.

Most importantly the group enjoyed our day away and our time together. Most everyone left feeling like we were on the right track and had accomplished a lot. The retreat succeeded in strengthening our bonds as a group and moving the program toward a brighter future.
❖

Community Conferencing Update

So, how are we doing? At this point, volunteers and staff working together in the CCNP community – the Stevens Square-Loring Heights, Loring Park, Elliot Park, and Downtown neighborhoods – have conferenced 29 incidents involving 31 offenders arrested for non-violent crimes in the downtown and surrounding area. The majority of our cases so far have dealt with Soliciting Prostitution, but we have also handled Trespassing, Open Bottle, Consuming in Public, Disorderly Conduct/Urination, and Felony Theft cases. The program is prepared to tackle other crimes, too: Vandalism/Graffiti, Panhandling, and Shoplifting are all priority concerns in our area. So far, the program has been able to conference all court-referred cases that meet the program criteria.

In dealing with the kinds of offenses that affect the quality of life in our neighborhoods, the 75+ people who have participated in these face-to-face discussions about impact and reintegration have worked toward outcomes that directly benefit the community: gardening, delivering meals to shut-ins, picking up litter, volunteering at Salvation Army, letters of apology, translation services, outreach to immigrants, charitable donations, and the list goes on.... Remarkably, 88% of our participants to date have successfully completed the program – meaning that they attended the conference, brought supporters, took ownership for their actions, worked out a reparative agreement, and followed through on that contract.

Community feedback (through surveys) indicates a high level of satisfaction with the process and outcomes. Almost 100% of survey respondents have responded "yes" to the questions "Were you satisfied with the outcome?" and "Do think that justice was served?" Here are a few of the comments we received from our last 4 cases:

- "In court (he) would have never realized that his actions could so effect others' lives!" (employee)
- "Very real consequences imposed, which the court doesn't handle well for this type of case." (corrections employee)

continued on page 3

114

Appreciation Dinner Celebrates Success!

At a special dinner recognizing our volunteers and supporters,
approximately 75 people from the community, police
department, churches, and local businesses gathered on
December 1st to celebrate the success of a year of Community
Conferencing. The guests enjoyed a buffet provided by the
City of Lakes Transitional Care Center, and then received
certificates for their contributions to the CCNP Restorative
Justice Program. The Minneapolis Downtown Council also
helped sponsor the event, which featured guest speakers Dan
Mabley, the Chief Judge of Hennepin County District Court,
and Susan Stacey, Restorative Justice Planner with the
Minnesota Department of Corrections.

Highlighting the significance of the CCNP experiment with
restorative justice, Ms. Stacey noted that CCNP's Community
Conferencing "is a model program – in the state, and
nationally." The guests, when asked what they gained through
their involvement in restorative justice, had many responses.
Community members talked about empowerment ("You can
participate in getting something done") and responsibility ("I
can't walk around with blinders on"). One local resident said
simply, "I like talking to the offender." Another said that
restorative justice is about building community, and making
people "feel more at home" in their neighborhood.

System professionals had something to say, too.
Neighborhood Probation Officer Jeff Bailey emphasized the
importance of reintegration, remarking that "they will come
back; this makes our job easier." Police talked about the
opportunity to get to know citizens in the community, and
letting the community get to know them. From the City
Attorney's Office, we heard that community involvement
creates bargaining power, showing judges and attorneys that
"these people care."

Thanks to everyone who has helped the CCNP community
create this experiment and strive, in one offender's words, "to
turn the negative into positive." ❖

Community Conferencing Steps

- Offender , victim, and supporters meet with community
  members in the neighborhood of the offense
- People take turns describing the impact of the behavior
- The group creates a reparative agreement, decided by
  consensus
- Offender makes amends to the victim and community

From the Desk of . . . Ray Paulson

Greetings! My name is Ray Paulson and I am the community
organizer for the CCNP Restorative Justice Program. I have a
few insights about this program, which I would like to share,
but first allow me to say a few words about myself. I am a
native Nebraskan and first came to Minnesota to go to school
at Macalester College. While there, I began my activism by
helping organize the Tenants Union for off-campus students. I
also worked for the Office of Multicultural Affairs on a
program to aid students of color adjust to college life, led the
recycling program, and affirmed my belief in rugby as the
supreme team sport.

After graduating with a degree in International Studies, I
signed up with Americorps*VISTA and moved to Austin,
Texas where I developed a program designed to help homeless
workers gain self-sufficiency. Like most things, this goal could
not be achieved in a vacuum. Organizing the clients and
other service providers was often a critical part of any positive
development. Furthermore, my involvement with the
homeless often brought me into contact with the criminal
justice system. This contact also gave me an awareness of
many shortcomings that make the system frustrating for
people on both sides of the law, in the homeless population
and the community at-large. This awareness has carried
through to my new position with the CCNP Restorative
Justice program.

In our quest to address low-level crimes in communal space,
we often hit homeless issues head on. Restorative Justice is
not always a perfect fit for homeless offenders, but traditional
criminal justice is not entirely appropriate either. The reason I
say this is because many would not be offenders if they were
not homeless and vice versa. While neither is a solution to
homelessness, Restorative Justice accomplishes something that
the court cannot. For the community, it demonstrates that
being homeless does not exempt a person from accepting
responsibility for his or her actions. Furthermore, the
reintegration philosophy of Restorative Justice does the
opposite of imprisonment and/or punishment. Instead of
alienating offenders and pushing them toward the edge of
society, it draws them in, emphasizing that even in offending
they are still part of our community.

After witnessing the isolation that many homeless folks
encounter just by virtue of being homeless, which is
compounded by the criminal justice system, I can confidently
say that Restorative Justice is a preferable alternative for all
involved. ❖

continued from page 1

Thank You!

We would like to thank the following people and organizations for their special contributions over the last three months:

- **Community Participants**: Jane Alexander and Heidi Carlsen from ProColor, Emily Andrews, Jeff Bailey, Delores Cotton, Sgt. Patricia Hellen and Off. Melissa Musich of the Mpls Police Dept., Marilyn Jackson, Dirk Larsen, Marie Listopad, Dr. Nicholas Long from Plymouth Church, Michael Lyght, Alexina Matanich of NSP, Carol Nichols from City of Lakes Transitional Care Center, Tim Nolan, Ron Staff of Stevens House, Arlene Storandt, and Karen Theis.
- **For coordinating service projects**, thanks to: City of Lakes Transitional Care Center (Margot Avey and Barbara Bluhm), Salvation Army (Pamela Bonesteel), Plymouth Church (Sue Garber), Stevens Square Community Organization Greening Program (Elise Kyllo and Berry Farrington), and the Minneapolis Police Department (Officer Melissa Musich).
- **For providing meeting space**, thanks to: Minneapolis Public Library, City of Lakes Transitional Care Center, First Covenant Church, Stevens Square-Loring Heights Probation Office, The Coyle – CCHT, Augustana Apartments, Our Lady of the Lake Church, and Elliot Park Recreation Center.
- **Conference Facilitators**: Angie Hugen, Karen Ives, David Madrigal, Becky Moyer, Ken Strobel, Sue Stacey
- **Interpreters**: Christine Langenfeld, Barbara Spencer
- **The Restorative Justice Advisory Team**: Sandra Anderson, John Balsa, Monroe Bell, Bev Hlavac, Jim Krahn, Brian Levy, Aaron Schlafly, Ken Strobel, JoAnn Ross, Scott Van Cleave, Dee Tvedt, and Sandra Westerdahl.

What Have You Done for Me Lately?

You may ask yourself, "What are we really getting out of Community Conferencing?" The easiest way to find a concrete answer: look at the records. Here are some agreements reached through conferencing over the past few months:

- A young man arrested for consuming in a downtown alley served lunches at Salvation Army (Currie Ave.) to visitors dropped off by the Detox Unit of the police department.
- For soliciting prostitution, one person is making $50 donations to PRIDE & Breaking Free; visiting a Spanish- speaking patient at a local nursing home; serving dinner at Plymouth Church; and writing a letter of apology to the arresting officer.
- After participating in a Community Conference for public urination, a program participant has written letters of apology to the Gay Nineties and Fire Station Ten (where he was arrested) and will spend 8 hours serving meals to the homeless.
- For soliciting prostitution, another person is writing a letter of apology to the church near the arrest site and has agreed to put in 30 hours community service with the neighborhood greening and gardening program. ❖

Conferencing Update

- "The community benefits from the offender, not the court system." (Minneapolis police officer)
- "I would have gotten fined and probably done the crime again." (offender)
- "There will be one more offender who doesn't have to go back to court." (resident)
- "This young man learned two important lessons: people care about the neighborhood and people care about him." (resident)
- "It seems pretty obvious that if (he) had been to the courts 4-5 times like he mentioned during the conference, the court system wasn't handling the situation very well, not to mention inefficiently." (employee)
- "Shame, which produces little, was transposed into positive action." (resident)
- "It makes me feel stronger to have a "voice" in the outcome...I got to say how I feel about my neighborhood." (resident)
- "Keep up the good work." (resident)

Not all cases have had the same level of success. So far, four people failed to complete their agreements or were arrested again for a same or similar offense; their cases were returned to the City Attorney's Office for prosecution. While discouraging for those community members who took the time to be involved, these interesting results are teaching us about what kind of restorative justice model really works for the community – for what kind of offender, and for what kind of offense. Three of the "failed" cases involved alcohol-related crimes, and all had a record of similar incidents, indicating a chronic problem. As a demonstration project, the Community Conferencing pilot program is delving into the unknown -- and no doubt has much to reveal.

What is success? Restorative justice is about much more than crime reduction, efficiency, and cost-effectiveness. When we are talking about "results" or "success," it is important to bear in mind that the objectives of restorative practices are different from, yet complementary to, the goals of the traditional criminal justice system. Whereas the traditional formal process is offender-oriented and focused on punishment and reducing recidivism, the restorative approach focuses on victim empowerment and healing, offender accountability, reparation, and reintegration. In addition to the fundamental objectives of restorative justice, we have placed an over-arching emphasis on community-building. Resolving quality-of-life crimes locally, reinforcing standards of behavior, and creating a "way back" for the offender is the kind of *public work* that citizens can effectively accomplish through collective effort. ❖

CCNP WINTER ACTIVITIES

- We have been busily expanding the reach of the program, working to develop a system whereby we can receive referrals from the Hennepin County Drug Court for Fifth degree possession. Look for more details later this Spring.

- The possibility of receiving cases from Operation de Novo for juveniles who commit crimes in the CCNP neighborhoods is also being investigated. If all goes well, we may see some referrals of this type in the coming months.

- CCNP also applauds efforts spearheaded by Rep. Karen Clark and Sen. Linda Berglin to appropriate funds for the MN Dept. of Corrections to be used for community-based programs and Restorative Justice training. If the bill passes, up to $4.1 million could be set aside for restorative justice in Minnesota.

- SHOPLIFTING is a crime that seriously impacts businesses. Let us know if this is a problem for you and would like help addressing the issue. Call 871-8100 for more information.

CALENDAR OF EVENTS

CCNP RJ POLICY COMMITTEE

PLACE: CITY OF LAKES TRANSITIONAL CARE CENTER
110 E. 18TH ST. (AUDITORIUM)
TIME: MARCH 29TH, 7:00 PM

We'll be discussing development of critical policy issues for the Community Conferencing program.

PROGRAM ORIENTATION

PLACE DOWNTOWN MINNEAPOLIS (CALL FOR LOCATION)
TIME: MARCH 22ND, 2:00 PM

Come learn the basics of Community Conferencing and find out how you can be a part of restorative justice in your neighborhood.

ADVISORY TEAM MEETING

PLACE: CITY OF LAKES TRANSITIONAL CARE CENTER
110 E. 18TH ST. (AUDITORIUM)
TIME APRIL 6TH, 7:00 PM

Meets the first Tuesday of every month. The Advisory Team steers the program and welcomes community input.

CCNP Restorative Justice Program

c/o Stevens Square Community Organization
110 East 18th St. # 112
Minneapolis, MN 55403
(612) 871-7107

ADDRESS CORRECTION REQUESTED

The *CCNP RJ Review* is a bi-monthly newsletter for the CCNP Restorative Justice Program. If you would like to volunteer more for the program, or want to be taken off of the mailing list, call (612) 871-8100 and talk to a staff person.

Hawke's Bay Restorative Justice Te Puna Wai Ora Inc.

CODE OF PRACTICE

A facilitator shall:

1 be non-judgmental and treat all parties with dignity and respect.

2 recognise and consider the different needs, values, cultural, religious and social beliefs of the tangata whenua and other participants.

3 work with integrity and skill in preparing participants for a conference.

4 facilitate the process of empowering the participants to find their own solutions while being aware of the issue of power imbalance and the need for physical and emotional safety.

5 monitor his/her own process with the assistance of the recorder and supervision in a way that is transparent to others

6 practise confidentiality and discretion at all times except when the demands of public good override the duty of confidentiality in the case of clear and serious risk to any person.

7 recognise the limits of his/her own professional competence and take responsibility for his/her own emotional/mental/physical health.

8 be responsible for developing relevant skills through further training.

9 acknowledge and challenge attitudes, values and beliefs which may be detrimental to effective facilitation.

10 have a responsibility to support other facilitators, respect differences and to act with integrity, honesty and courtesy. Sharing resources, ideas and experiences will promote the development in methodology of effective facilitation.

11 have clear boundaries between professional responsibilities and personal interests.

12 be clear about the limits of the role of a facilitator.

The management committee shall:

1 be clear about their role according to the Constitution.

2 abide by the sections of this code of practice which are relevant to this role.

3 provide the support necessary for facilitators to have the maximum opportunity to comply with the codes of ethics and practice.

Hawke's Bay Restorative Justice Te Puna Wai Ora Inc.

COMPLAINTS PROCEDURE

This procedure is available to facilitators, management committee and all who request and take part in community group conferences.

The management committee shall appoint a complaints committee comprising a minimum of three members, one of whom is appointed the convenor.

Should any member of the complaints committee be the subject of a complaint or have any personal involvement in the matter being investigted, they must declare their involvement and withdraw. Another person shall be appointed by the management committee for the duraton of the investigation.

All complaints are to be forwarded to the convenor of the complaints committee, who will within 7 days of receipt, send copies of the complaint to all members of the complaints committee and the person/s named in the complaint, acknowledging such action to the complainant.

Any facilitator or HBRJ member named in the complaint shall provide a written reply to the convenor of the complaints committee within 7 days of receipt of a copy of the complaint. The convenor will forward copies of this response to members of the complaints committee and the complainant.

If a satisfactory conclusion cannot be reached at this stage, the convenor will arrange a meeting with the complaints committee, the complainant and person/s named in the complaint (together with support people for both parties if desired).

If agreement is not reached at this time, a decision will be made by the complaints committee who will convey their decision in writing to all parties, the convenor of HBRJ management committee and the honorary solicitor within 7 days from the date of the meeting.

The convenor of the complaints committee shall record all complaints in a complaints register.

All documents relating to complaints are to be kept in a central file held by the convenor of the complaints committee.

Note:
a) The complaints committee shall decide if any person who is the subject of a complaint should be temporarily withdrawn from facilitation or any other duties he/she performs in positions held.

b) All involved should be aware of legislation which may be applicable in the particular circumstances i.e. the Human Rights Act 1993, the Victim of Offences Act 1987 and the Employment Contracts Act 1991.

Hawke's Bay
Restorative Justice
Te Puna Wai Ora Inc.

CODE OF ETHICS

1. To recognise the value and dignity of all persons irrespective of culture, status, gender, age, education, beliefs or contribution to society.

2. To honour the Treaty of Waitangi.

3. To believe that people are capable of taking responsibility for their behaviour and actions.

4. To abide by the principle of free and informed consent of clients in conferencing.

5. To trust the conference process to empower offenders, victims and others to find their own solutions where this is possible.

6. To believe in the need for professionalism and the continuing development of qualities and skills.

7. To uphold the principles of confidentiality except when a person's safety is threatened.

8. To believe in the right of all parties to be free from any kind of exploitation or harassment.

****

RESTORATIVE JUSTICE/COMMUNITY PROBATION SERVICE – LIASON/REFERAL PROTOCOLS

1   Referrals can be made at any stage ie Pre-Sentence or while person is serving a sentence (including prison sentence).

2   Referral is made on Restorative Justice referral form. Restorative Justice Facilitator may contact PO for further information if required. Probation Officer can also contact facilitator if they feel it necessary. If Probation Officer has relevant information re Reparation, sentencing options, this information needs to be given to Restorative Justice Facilitator so that the Restorative Justice process can compliment Court process.

3   Who contacts victim?   Depends on the situation – could be Probation Officer, Restorative Justice facilitator, Victim Support, Victim Advisor (available in Napier Court only). Discuss with Restorative Justice Convenor if necessary.

4   Role of Probation Officer in process – minimal. Strength of Restorative Justice process lies in it being a community initiative. In most cases it would not be appropriate for Probation Officer to attend. If Probation Officer does attend it should be only if invited, this is at the discretion of the facilitator.   Probation Officer to abide by ethical confidentiality guidelines of Restorative Justice.

5   Restorative Justice will provide a report to referring agency/person.

6   Probation Officer to report back to Restorative Justice after sentencing.

7   Review – where relevant Restorative Justice will report back to Probation Officer after a time agreed to by the conference as to whether agreement has been adhered to.

8   If Probation Officer has any concerns about Restorative Justice group/process, then Probation Officer to contact the Convenor of Restorative Justice. If the facilitator has concerns about the actions of a Probation Officer he/she is to contact the Community Probation liaison officer. (Frances Melody or George Henderson). Both agencies have complaint procedures, which can be used if necessary.

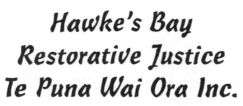 

Hawke's Bay Restorative Justice Te Puna Wai Ora Inc.

COMMUNITY GROUP CONFERENCE REPORT FORM

Referral #

Name of offender

Name of victim

Offence

Date and place of meeting

Others in attendance

Outcome	Signatures
Follow-up plan	
Facilitator	

Hawke's Bay
Restorative Justice
Te Puna Wai Ora Inc.

To empower all people affected by crime or personal harm to work towards restoration, reconciliation and healing

P O Box 1495   HASTINGS
Phone 877 8889   Fax 877 4169

Restorative Justice

- focuses on accountability and repairing the harm instead of retribution and punishment

- enables the offender to be directly responsible to the victim

- offers an opportunity for the victim's needs to be met

- transfers power from the state to the community

- gives a better deal to victims by bringing them from the edge into the heart of the process.

It is important that:

- participants want to be involved attendance is voluntary

- participants are informed about the process

- expectations are realistic

- the process is fair and safe for all participants

- the conference content is confidential, unless there is serious risk to any person

Facing the victim is no soft option for the offender.

If you have any questions, wish to offer your support or would like to use this service please phone 877 8889

123

What is Restorative Justice?

It is a process which offers an opportunity:

- for victims of crime or personal harm to tell their story and have their questions answered

- for offenders to take responsibility for what they have done and offer to make amends

- for victims to have a say in how offenders may repair the harm done

- for all those affected to participate in this process

This is a time when reconciliation and healing may begin.

How does this happen?

- Victims, offenders and other affected people are invited to take part in a community group conference held in a neutral place.

When can a conference be held?

- when a victim or offender requests a conference.

- when an offender admits an offence and the police choose diversion

- between conviction and sentencing in the District Court process

- before release from prison

- outside the criminal justice system

Who runs the conference?

- trained facilitators who are required to abide by the codes of ethics, practice and procedures of Hawkes Bay Restorative Justice Te Puna Wai Ora Inc. Copies of these are available on request.

What will happen at the conference?

- The offender and the victim will be asked to describe the incident and how they have been affected by it.

- Other participants are invited to describe how the incident has affected them.

- This is an opportunity for the offender to face the effects of his/her actions and accept responsibility for these.

- Discussion takes place about how the offender can repair the harm done.

- Everyone at the conference must agree about this. The facilitator guides this process.

- Decisions are recorded and copies sent to conference participants and any referral agency. Arrangements are made to follow up the conference outcome.

Hawke's Bay Restorative Justice Te Puna Wai Ora Inc.

To empower all people affected by crime or personal harm to work towards restoration, reconciliation and healing

P O Box 1495   HASTINGS
Phone 877 8889   Fax 877 4169

Participants Rights and Responsibilities

It is important that ....

- you want to be involved - attendance is voluntary

- your expectations are realistic

- you say what you think and feel - it is okay to be angry or sad

- everyone is allowed to have their say without interruption

- there are no put downs, threats or abuse - verbal or physical

- different views are respected

- conference content is confidential - what is said stays there - unless there is a serious risk to any person

- the process is fair and safe for all involved

If you don't understand - ask

What do I do if I am concerned about the way I was treated or how the conference was organised or run?

- You may contact a member of the independent ethics committee at the number below.

- Any participant of a conference can file a written complaint.

- Complaints are dealt with by the ethics committee. You will be informed of the process.

- If you are not sure what to do or have any questions please phone 877 8889

Participants are entitled to be treated fairly and respectfully by the facilitator and any other members of the organisation

125

What is Restorative Justice?

It is a process which offers an opportunity:

• for victims of crime or personal harm to tell their story and have their questions answered

• for offenders to take responsibility for what they have done and offer to make amends

• for victims to have a say in how offenders may repair the harm done

• for all those affected to participate in this process

This is a time when reconciliation and healing may begin.

How does this happen?

• Victims, offenders and other affected people are invited to take part in a community group conference held in a neutral place.

When can a conference be held?

• when a victim or offender requests a conference.

• when an offender admits an offence and the police choose diversion

• between conviction and sentencing in the District Court process

• before release from prison

• outside the criminal justice system

Who runs the conference?

• trained facilitators who are required to abide by the codes of ethics, practice and procedures of Hawkes Bay Restorative Justice Te Puna Wai Ora Inc. Copies of these are available on request.

What will happen at the conference?

• The offender and the victim will be asked to describe the incident and how they have been affected by it.

• Other participants are invited to describe how the incident has affected them.

• This is an opportunity for the offender to face the effects of his/her actions and accept responsibility for these.

• Discussion takes place about how the offender can repair the harm done.

• Everyone at the conference must agree about this. The facilitator guides this process.

• Decisions are recorded and copies sent to conference participants and any referral agency. Arrangements are made to follow up the conference outcome.

Hawke's Bay Restorative Justice Te Puna Wai Ora Inc.

PROCEDURES

Conference arrangements

1. Hawkes Bay Restorative Justice Te Puna Wai Ora Inc will only accept applications for conferences made on the prescribed referral form and deemed suitable by the allocation subgroup of the management committee.

2. The allocation subgroup shall select the appropriate facilitator for the conference bearing in mind the relevant characteristics and location of the parties, the skills and experience required of the facilitator and the fair distribution of cases between suitable facilitators.

3. A facilitator shall only accept a conference he/she believes is appropriate for him/her and the participants.

4. Conferences will only be held in cases when the offender freely admits personal responsibility for the offence and acknowledges that there is harm to repair. If he/she later retracts the admission the conference shall be terminated.

5. The facilitator shall describe the conference process and discuss its possible consequences with the victim and the offender before confirming their consent to participate. This may involve personal visits. He/she shall respect the decision of a prospective participant who declines to attend.

6. The victim is invited to attend the conference only after the offender has agreed to come. If the victim is unwilling/unable to attend he/she can nominate another person to attend the conference in his/her place.

7. The facilitator shall consult the victim and the offender about who else will be invited to attend the conference. All participants shall receive information about the process, their rights and responsibilities, and the practical arrangements.

8. The conference shall be carefully and appropriately planned. The needs and choices of the victim are to be given paramount consideration.

9. Participants shall be informed of the limits of confidentiality. If danger to another person requires the facilitator to consider breaking confidentiality he/she shall endeavour to consult with a supervisor or a member of the ethics committee (unless this compromises immediate safety). If disclosure is deemed necessary the facilitator shall, if appropriate, seek the cooperation of the particular participant.

Professional practice

21. Facilitators require a knowledge of other community services to enable them to provide appropriate information when participants require other assistance.

22. Facilitators shall express concerns about a colleague in a professional manner, either directly to the colleague, in clinical supervision, or through the complaints procedure.

23. Facilitators must complete the organisation's training course and be selected by the formal selection process. Appointments will be reviewed annually.

24. Facilitators are required to attend regular clinical and peer supervision and should request individual supervision for serious issues (available at the discretion of the ethics committee.)

25. Facilitators are to attend regular training and take other opportunities to increase their knowledge and skills.

26. Facilitators shall abide by the organisation's codes of ethics and practice.

Management responsibilities

27. The management committee of Hawkes Bay Restorative Justice Te Puna Wai Ora Inc. shall provide the relevant structures to support these procedures, including the provision of an ethics committee, complaints procedure, ongoing training and supervision, in consultation with the facilitators.

28. The management committee shall provide a framework to further develop the codes of ethics and practice, and procedures, in consultation with facilitator representatives.

29. The management committee shall develop an evaluation process for conference participants and collect relevant statistics which can be used to assess the value of the service.

****

PIEDMONT DISPUTE RESOLUTION CENTER

ACCOUNTABILITY CONFERENCE

AGREEMENT

PDRC Case #:_____ Incident date:_____ Juvenile_____

I will complete the following, which have been agreed to at this Conference today.

1. A personal apology to the victim	YES/NO	Victim will contact Rappahanock Juvenile Court Services,
2. A written apology to the victim	YES/NO	(540) 347-8634 or (540) 675-3888, when agreement is completed.
3. Compensation/Reparation	YES/NO	Signature of Victim_____
4. Plan for monitoring completion	YES/NO	Date_____

5. Other matters, including monitoring plan:

_____

_____

_____

_____

_____

_____

I agree to the above _____Youth

Witnessed and agreed _____Parent/Guardian/Supporter

Witnessed and agreed _____Victim

Witness_____Probation Officer/Police

Other witnesses_____   _____

_____   _____   _____

_____   _____   _____

_____   _____   _____

Location of Conference_____   Date_____

Conference Facilitator_____

Piedmont Dispute Resolution Center * P.O. Box 809 * Warrenton, Virginia 20188-0809 * (540) 347-6650

FLOW CHART -- COMMUNITY ACCOUNTABILITY CONFERENCING
FAUQUIER JUVENILE & DOMESTIC RELATIONS DISTRICT COURT
Dispositional Group Originating from Court
From Referral to Conference

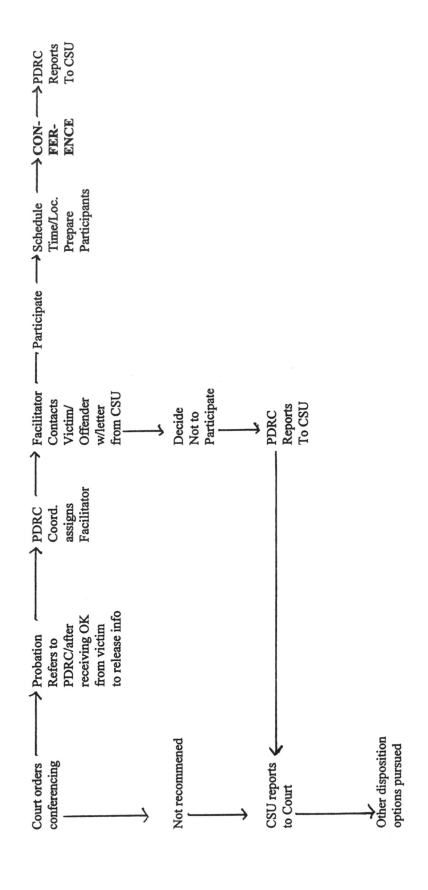

Court orders conferencing → Probation Refers to PDRC/after receiving OK from victim to release info → PDRC Coord. assigns Facilitator → Facilitator Contacts Victim/ Offender w/letter from CSU → Participate → Schedule Time/Loc. Prepare Participants → CON-FER-ENCE → PDRC Reports To CSU

Decide Not to Participate → PDRC Reports To CSU

Not recommened → CSU reports to Court → Other disposition options pursued

3/98-PDRC

FLOW CHART -- COMMUNITY ACCOUNTABILITY CONFERENCING
FAUQUIER JUVENILE & DOMESTIC RELATIONS DISTRICT COURT
Dispositional Group Originating from Court
From Conference to Outcome

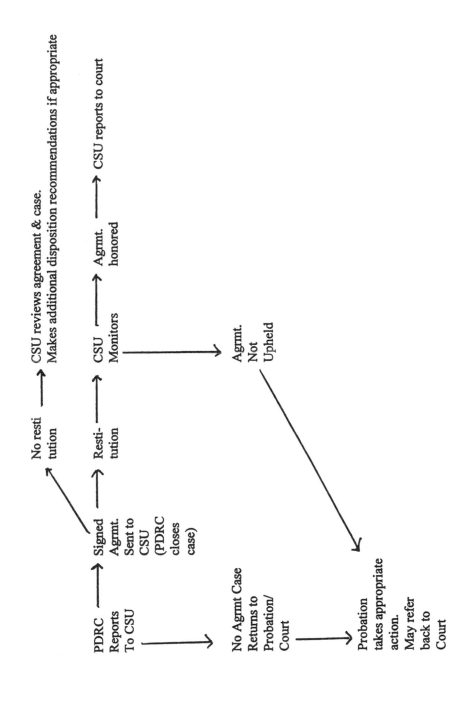

PDRC Reports To CSU → Signed Agrmt. Sent to CSU (PDRC closes case) → No restitution → CSU reviews agreement & case. Makes additional disposition recommendations if appropriate

Restitution → CSU Monitors → Agrmt. honored → CSU reports to court

CSU Monitors → Agrmt. Not Upheld

No Agrmt Case Returns to Probation/ Court → Probation takes appropriate action. May refer back to Court

3/98-PDRC

PIEDMONT DISPUTE RESOLUTION CENTER
P.O. Box 809
Warrenton, Virginia 20188
(540) 347-6650

CONSENT TO RELEASE/EXCHANGE INFORMATION

Regarding:_____   _____

_____   _____

I wish to be considered for participation in the REAL JUSTICE Accountability Conferencing Program administered by the Piedmont Dispute Resolution Center and understand that information about me and the events and circumstances which will be the subject of the conference may be assembled.

I authorize the Piedmont Dispute Resolution Center to receive and exchange confidential information if and when necessary and for professional purposes only to and from: the Culpeper Juvenile Probation Department.

This authorization may be revoked at any time by submitting a request in writing.

_____   _____
Victim's Signature   Date

_____   _____
Victim's Parent/Guardian Signature if under 18 years old   Date

_____   _____
Youth's Signature   Date

_____   _____
Parent/Guardian's Signature   Date

_____   _____
Witness Signature and Title   Date

6/98--PDRC

132

YOUTH ACCOUNTABILITY CONFERENCING PROGRAM AT PIEDMONT DISPUTE RESOLUTION CENTER

Vision:
- To provide a cost-effective new approach to juvenile crime
- To provide a quality program that serves the victims and offenders of juvenile crime, to encourage accountability and repair harm done to victims
- To promote community participation in the prevention of juvenile crime
- To provide an alternative to current forms of punishment and restitution in the juvenile justice system

Principles:
Restorative justice:

- Accountability/shame
- Understanding
- Empathy
- Forgiveness
- Restitution
- Reconciliation
- Reintegration

Community building:
- Support
- Encouragement
- Moral learning
- Bridge building between adults and juveniles
- Peace

Conditions:
- Offenders must admit guilt
- Participation of victims is always voluntary
- Participation of offender is voluntary unless court ordered

Types of cases Conferenced:
- Truancy
- Assault
- Petty larceny
- Disruptive behavior
- Shoplifting

"victimless crimes"
speeding
reckless driving
possession of alcohol
possession of marijuana

PIEDMONT DISPUTE RESOLUTION CENTER
P.O. Box 809
Warrenton, Virginia 20188-0809
(540) 347-6650

ACCOUNTABILITY CONFERENCING CONSENT FORM

An Accountability Conference offers victims and offenders and their community of support an opportunity to meet in a safe, confidential environment, with the help of a neutral facilitator. During the Conference, victims, offenders and their support persons can talk openly about their feelings and how they need the harm caused by the juvenile's actions repaired.

We understand that the facilitators do not impose their values or make suggestions about what they think should be in an agreement. Only participants themselves can make the terms of the agreement.

We understand that we can at any time and for any reason choose another alternative such as the court system.

We understand and agree that everything said during the conference is confidential. There are two exceptions: allegations of child abuse and/or neglect or a threat of future harm. We further understand that if we reach a signed agreement, that agreement will be sent to the probation department.

We also understand and agree not to involve the staff, facilitators, or records of PDRC in any court proceeding whatsoever and waive our right to sue these parties.

We also understand that we may have certain legal rights under the law and if any of us would like them explained, we will seek legal advice elsewhere. Participants can have an attorney review the agreement before signing it.

We agree to carry out the agreement if the conference results in a written agreement.

Signature of victim_____

Signature of offender_____

Signature of offender's
parents/guardians_____

Signatures of others present_____

_____

_____

_____

_____

Date_____

2/98-PDRC

134

Initial Interview

Name_____

Date_____

Date of Conference_____

Facilitator_____

1. What would you like to see come out of this conference?

2. What would you like to see the offenders do or what would you like to see happen to them?

3. If you were at the conference, what would you most likely want to say?

4. **Who has been affected by the incident outside of yourself?**

5. **In what way has this affected your family?**

6. What is the most threatening thing about attending the conference?

7. What outcome from the conference would help you to heal and put this behind you?

8. What would help you feel safe again?

9. Have you ever wondered why the incident happened?

10. Is there someone in your family or community who is willing to attend the conference? Phone #?

11. Do you have any questions about the conference process?

12. Do you understand that it is your choice to participate or not?

Checklist

Do I have a clear understanding of the incident?

Have you invited everyone who could or should be present?

Do all participants understand the purpose and process of the conference?
Date
Time
Location

ACCOUNTABILITY CONFERENCING PROGRAM

PIEDMONT DISPUTE RESOLUTION CENTER
P.O. Box 809
Warrenton, Virginia 20188-0809
(540) 347-6650

REFERRAL FORM

Referred by_____

Date_____Time_____

Juvenile's Name_____

       Address_____

       _____

Father/Step/
Guardian's Name_____

       Address_____

       _____

Mother/Step/
Guardian's Name_____

       Address_____

       _____

Victim's Name _____

       Address_____

       _____

Date of offense_____

Nature of Offense_____

_____

Other Information_____

_____

_____

Return Court Date:_____

Phone:_____

Grade_____School_____

Phone_____

Age_____Sex_____

Phone (h)_____

      (w)_____

Phone (h)_____

      (w)_____

Phone (h)_____

      (w)_____

**Attach signed release form

DATE: _____

TO: _____

FROM: _____

CASE NUMBER: PDRC _____ COURT: _____

CASE NAME: _____

CASE TYPE: _____

RETURN DATE: _____

The center reports to the Court that an Accountability Conference was scheduled for the above parties and:

( ) all parties participated in the Conference and reached an agreement which they wish to submit to the court to have entered as a court order (see attached)

( ) all parties participated in the Conference and reached an agreement which they have taken to their attorneys for review

( ) all parties participated in the Conference. It is our understanding that the victim will be contacting the court relevant to the disposition of the case

( ) all parties participated in the Conference but did not reach an agreement

( ) one or more parties did not attend the scheduled Conference

( ) one or more parties exercised their option of withdrawing from the Conference

( ) our attempts to schedule a Conference were unsuccessful

( ) parties participated in the Conference and were informed that they are to appear in Court on their return date

PDRC 2/99

PIEDMONT DISPUTE RESOLUTION CENTER
P.O. BOX 809
WARRENTON, VIRGINIA 20188-0809
(540) 347-6650

ACCOUNTABILITY CONFERENCING REPORT

DATE: _____

TO: _____

FROM: _____

STUDENT NAME: _____

       The Center reports to the school that an Accountability Conference and/or a Truancy Conference was scheduled for the above parties and:

       ( ) all parties participated in the Conference and reached an agreement which they wish to submit to the school (see attached agreement)

       ( ) all parties participated in the Conference but did not reach an agreement

       ( ) one or more parties did not attend the Conference

       ( ) our attempts to schedule a Conference were not successful

       ( ) other: _____

PDRC 12/98

Flow Chart--Accountability Conferencing Time Line for Facilitators & Coordinator from Referral to Survey Collection

Referral to PDRC

2 days

PDRC Coordinator assigns Facilitator

1. Facilitator contacts Victim/offender
2. Facilitator schedules initial interview within one week
3. Facilitators contacts Coordinator w/questions & schedule.

one week

1. Initial interviews completed.
2. Conference scheduled.
3. Facilitator contacts support persons & prepares for Conference.
4. Status call to Coordinator with questions/scheduling.

one week

CONFERENCE

PDRC Coordinator reports to referral source.

2 days

PDRC Coordinator sends our Thank you letters.

2 days

PDRC Coordinator checks on surveys.

one week

Victim or Offender declined to participate

or

Facilitator recommends against Conferencing at this time.

PDRC Coordinator reports back to referral source.

2 days

Action taken by Referral Source.

Approximately 2 week duration from assignment to Facilitator to Conference.

Conferencing "victimless crimes":

What is a victimless crime?
A victimless crime is one that has no *direct* victim. Examples of these types of cases would be: reckless driving, speeding, possession of alcohol or marijuana, or destruction of public property.

Who represents the victim at the Conference?
We see the community, (as well as the offender themselves) as the victim. A community representative will attend the Conference and act as a victim would. They will speak about how this type of crime has effected their lives in the past, either as a victim or as an offender. They may be professionals such as policemen and rescue workers who see the results of these types of crimes every day. This is a chance for moral learning, education and accountability for the offender who may not understand how his or her actions could possibly effect others.

How does the shaming process work in these Conferences?
These Conferences can be as emotional an experience as any typical Conference. The community representatives sometimes have just as much anger, pain, etc... as any victim of a crime may have. This is good, because the "reintegrative-shame" concept is brought forth in a somewhat different form, but it is just as effective as if there were a direct victim involved. The juvenile still has to face his family and these community representatives and that experience personalizes the crime, causing the shaming that leads to accountability, and ultimately to reconciliation and reintegration.

Is the script used in these cases?
Yes, we follow the script in all cases. Some small change may need to be made to address the participants involved. That should be done on a case by case basis. *For example:* (community representative) Mr. Smith, can you tell us how your life was effected when you were badly injured in the accident that you had last year as a result of speeding ?-- instead of, (actual victim) How has *this* incident effected you?

What happens in the agreement phase?
The agreement can be as creative as in a typical Conference. A community representative may suggest the offender do some community service at a rescue squad or similar place, may bring literature along for the offender to read (anti-drug use handouts, public service messages etc...) or simply request that the offender write a letter to the community apologizing for the crime. Sometimes you may have an agreement that

2

simply states that the offender understands how speeding can impact lives and the community. The offender and the community representatives come up with the agreement together. (The community representatives may need some "coaching" on this before the Conference.) The agreement is signed and everyone participating receives a copy.

How does the facilitator locate community representatives?
The facilitator may know someone that might be a good community representative, a personal friend or a neighbor. Police departments, fire and rescue stations, hospitals, storeowners would be appropriate. Any person that works and/or lives in the community could be a community representative. If one of these types of crimes has impacted their lives or they work in a field where they experience the impact of these crimes, they will make good community representatives. Other facilitators that have Conferenced these types of cases would also be good resources for locating community representatives.

- *The same process is used in preparing for a victimless crime case as would be done for a typical case. Meeting with the offender and the community representative is an important part of the Conference process.*

Suggestions for amending script to use in Conferencing victimless crimes

I.   ***introduction*** --- use regular script:
     introduce participants, state the reason that the community representative is participating, his or her employment, personal experience etc...

II. ***offender*** --- use regular script

III. ***victim --- community representative #1***: *police or fire and rescue person*
     Key questions:
     - Can you tell us how your experience in dealing with this type of crime might benefit us in this Conference today?
     - What is the reaction of family members of offenders when you confront them about this type of incident?
     - Who is effected when this type of crime occurs?

     Community representative #2: *victim of a similar crime, or someone that has experienced the effects of this type of crime*
     Key questions:
     - Can you share with us the incident that occurred in your life that has brought you here today?
     - What was your reaction at the time of the incident?
     - How did you feel about what happened?
     - What has happened for you since the incident?
     - How did your family and friends react when they heard about the incident?

     ** *These questions are suggestions. They may be altered depending on your community representatives.*

IV. ***victim supporters*** --- in most cases there won't be any community representative supporters, if there is a support person (as in the case of a victim of a similar crime) you would use the regular script
     Example: How did you feel about what happened to your friend?

V.   ***offenders supporters*** --- use regular script

VI. ***agreement*** --- use regular script
     community representatives may make suggestions

VII. ***closing the conference*** --- use regular script

Conferencing Truancy

The Accountability Conferencing process for Truancy cases is generally the same as is done for victimless crimes. The regular script is followed, using the amendments provided for victimless crimes.

Meeting with the offender (and his or her families) is important to help them to understand what Accountability Conferencing is and why PDRC is involved in a "school issue."

One difference would be a school representative attending the Conference instead of a community representative. When choosing a school representative to attend the Conference, it is important to choose someone that the student likes and respects (as a support person *and* as a school official.)

Often the student has many concerns about certain school officials, and it is not productive to have those people as *support* persons. However, if there are issues with a specific school official, it is important to include them in the Conference in order to decide how to get that situation resolved, get the student back into school and repair the harm done to the school community and to the offender himself. In this case it is important to include that official *and* another school official that will serve as a support person for the offender. *Having support persons that work at the school—teachers, principles, volunteer tutors, etc... is important in these Conferences to foster an atmosphere of caring and reconciliation.* The offender may also invite any other support persons he or she would like to attend the Conference.

Meeting with the offender will help in deciding what school officials should attend the Conference.

The agreement phase will vary with each case, just as with regular Conferencing. Here are some suggestions in *preparing* the school and the offender for this phase of the Conference:

Ask the school what they can offer the student as an incentive to attend school.

Ask the offender what he or she thinks would make it easier for them to attend school more regularly.

Ask the family and support persons of the offender to think of ways that they could help get the offender to school.

The agreement is turned into the school and considered "official." This means that if the student does not honor the agreement, the case will be referred to the court.

TRUANCY CONFERENCING
at
Piedmont Dispute Resolution Center

Dear

      You and your child, _____, have been referred to Truancy Conferencing at the Piedmont Dispute Resolution Center (PDRC) to work out an agreement that keeps your child in school. *Finding ways to resolve truancy may reduce the possibility of further action being taken against you.*

      During a Truancy Conference you and your child will meet together with a school representative in a relaxed, confidential atmosphere to discuss your child's truancy from school and its impact on those involved. The Conference will be conducted by a trained, neutral volunteer from the Piedmont Dispute Resolution Center. People who are your fellow-citizens are the facilitators; they do not take sides or tell you what to do. They are there to help you decide for yourself how to resolve the problem.

      You are also encouraged to have other support persons present at the Conference, such as a grandparent, aunt, uncle, siblings, friends, minister, coach, etc. The Conference may also be attended by a representative from the community. The facilitator will talk to you and your child before the conference to help you decide who else should attend.

      If an agreement is reached, your child will sign an Agreement Form which indicates his/her commitment to uphold their part of the agreement. The form will also be signed by everyone else at the Conference. The form is not legally binding and does not affect your legal rights.

      In many cases, youth who attend a Truancy Conference gain a greater understanding of the gravity of the situation.

      To schedule a Truancy Conference, or if you have any questions about the program, call Mrs. Vickie Shoap, Youth Accountability Conferencing Coordinator at PDRC, (540) 347-6650.

      The Piedmont Dispute Resolution Center is a community-based, non-profit organization and a Piedmont United Way Agency. ***There is no cost for this service.***

CASE # _____

WOODBURY POLICE DEPARTMENT
FAMILY GROUP CONFERENCING
REPARATION AGREEMENT

OFFENDER NAME: _____

_____

_____

_____

OFFENSE: _____

VICTIM NAME: _____

_____

_____

_____

OFFENSE DATE: _____ CONFERENCE DATE: _____

The above named individuals agree upon the following as reparation:

Terms of this agreement must be fully completed by: _____
Failure to complete the terms of this agreement may result in further legal consequenses for the offender.

OFFENDER: _____ DATE: _____

VICTIM: _____ DATE: _____

COORDINATOR: _____ DATE: _____

DATE AGREEMENT SATISFIED: _____

RESTJUST\REPAGREE

2100 Radio Drive • Woodbury, Minnesota 55125-9598 • 612/739-4141 • FAX 714-3708 (**POLICE**)
612/714-3700 • FAX 714-3703 (**FIRE**)

DEPARTMENT OF PUBLIC SAFETY
POLICE/FIRE/EMERGENCY MEDICAL SERVICES

NOTICE OF ACTION ON JUVENILE CASE

Mr./Ms._____   Re: C#_____

_____

_____

On _____ your son/daughter _____ was
involved in an incident of _____ in Woodbury, MN.
The incident was investigated by Officer _____. It has been
determined that the case will be:

☐ Sent to the prosecutor for prosecution through the regular criminal
justice/court system. The prosecutor's office will notify you of case
information. You should direct questions to the Washington County
Attorney's Office, Juvenile Division at (651) 430-6115 .

☐ Assigned to a community diversion conferencing program. You will be
contacted by a conference facilitator within ten (10) days.

☐ A juvenile citation has been issued and a copy has been sent to the
county attorney's office. They will contact you regarding the case.
Questions should be directed to the Washington County Attorney,
Juvenile Division at (651) 430-6115.

☐ A Juvenile Warning has been issued and a copy is attached to this form.
The warning is kept on file in our office and the county prosecutor's
office. Accumulation of additional warnings may require further action
by the prosecutor. You are not required to take any action at this time.

☐ A Juvenile Warning has been issued and a referral made to another
agency for additional intervention. Failure to contact that referral
agency and complete any assigned program will result in further action,
including the option of prosecution.

Call the Woodbury Police at (651) 739-4141 for any needed clarification of this
information.

WE HELP
The Woodbury Way

RESTORATIVE

JUSTICE

Conference
Time:
Date:
Place:

Conferencing restores people and builds community

For more information call
Woodbury Police Department
739-4141

For more information call
Woodbury Police Department
739-4141

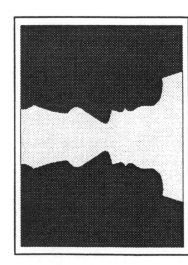

Juvenile crime is growing faster than population. Even in a city growing as rapidly as Woodbury this statement holds true. FBI Director Louis Freeh has warned that juvenile crime may well be the greatest crisis facing America as we enter the next century.

Traditional methods of handling juvenile crime do not appear to be working very effectively. Often the system takes way too long to confront an offender. It offers no mechanism for victim involvement and most often fails to address an offender's need to reintegrate into the community. It can leave an offender feeling isolated and permanently labeled as a bad person. This can actually increase the likelihood of re-offending. Victims are left with no closure to the incident, feeling an increase of fear and often isolation from the community.

Restorative Justice programs attempt to solve these problems at the community level through direct interaction of the victim, the offender and the community.

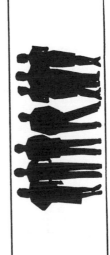

The Woodbury Police began conferencing in May of 1995. Our post conference evaluations indicate most participants are very satisfied with the conference and its outcome. Cases are conferenced based on a set of criteria that include:

1) Seriousness of the offense
2) Attitude of the offender
3) Attitude of the offender's parents
4) Past record of the offender

Along with these four criteria, the overall circumstances of each incident are also considered. Once a conference is completed and the agreement satisfied, the case is closed with no further action taken.

Juvenile crimes and problems occur in the community, in our own neighborhoods. Conferencing allows us to solve these problems and deal with our children in our community; our neighborhoods, where these children will continue to live and grow. It allows this community to directly impact its children and their behaviors. It helps build community by bringing people together to solve problems and reach mutual conclusions.

Woodbury Police Department's Community Conferencing Program sends qualified juvenile offenders to a community conference instead of court. While not all offenders or circumstances fit this model, many work well within this concept. In some cases, traditional court may still be deemed more appropriate and more effective.

Our program invites victims and offenders, along with their families, friends and neighbors to meet in a safe, controlled setting to discuss the incident and how it affected each person participating in the conference. A specially trained Woodbury officer facilitates the conference allowing the victim and offender to reach a mutual agreement that restores the victim and re-integrates the offender to the community. Our officers do not counsel or dictate agreements. We act only as moderators, providing a safe environment for everyone to express their feelings and achieve closure to the incident. We monitor all agreements to make sure they are completely fulfilled in a timely manner. Conferences are always voluntary for both the victim and offender. Traditional court options are still possible in lieu of conferencing.

RESTORATIVE JUSTICE QUESTIONNAIRE

Case # _____

Scale: 1=Lowest Score, 10=Highest Score

Rate your over all satisfaction with the conference:

    1   2   3   4   5   6   7   8   9   10

Rate the process as to how fairly you were treated:

    1   2   3   4   5   6   7   8   9   10

Rate the process as to how fairly everyone else involved was treated:

    1   2   3   4   5   6   7   8   9   10

Do you feel participating in the Restorative Justice was preferable to having your situation handled by the court system?

                 YES   NO

Are there things that you think the court system could have accomplished in this situation that the conference couldn't or didn't?

                 YES   NO   What?_____

If faced with a similar situation in the future, would you choose the Restorative Justice Program over the court system?

                 YES   NO

Please add any comments and/or suggestions you may have.

_____

_____

_____

_____

WOODBURY PUBLIC SAFETY
RESTORATIVE JUSTICE
COMMUNITY CONFERENCE SUMMARY
A participant list must accompany this summary. All officers attending (except facilitator) must be listed !

Incident_____ Date_____ C#_____

Date/Time of conference_____ Length (time) of conference_____

# of police personnel present_____ # of non-police persons present_____
Name officers present_____

# of Juvenile offenders present_____	# of Victims present_____
# of Offender supporters present_____	# of Victim supporters present_____
Relationships_____	Relationships_____

Disposition:_____
_____
_____
_____
_____

Referrals:____YSB ___HSI ____Family Links ____Other:_____

Followup:_____
_____
_____
_____

Officer Overtime: Facilitator (total time)_____ Other officers (total time)_____
(if none indicate by None or ∅) Name(s)_____

Victim letter (eval.) sent_____ Offender letter (eval.) sent_____

Total prep time on conference_____

Is there a written agreement_____ Due date_____

Conference facilitator_____ Date_____

Days between offense/conference_____ Days between assignment/conference_____

Agreement satisfied (date)_____ Restitution paid Y N Partial
                                           Explain partial payments_____
                                           _____
                                           _____

151

2100 Radio Drive • Woodbury, Minnesota 55125-9598 • 612/739-4141 • FAX 714-3708 (*POLICE*)
612/714-3700 • FAX 714-3703 (*FIRE*)

DEPARTMENT OF PUBLIC SAFETY
POLICE/FIRE/EMERGENCY MEDICAL SERVICES

Dear Restorative Justice Conference Participant:

This letter has been provided to help answer some questions and help prepare you for the scheduled family group conference. The Woodbury Police Department's experience with the conferencing has been positive and rewarding. Throughout this process, we welcome your thoughts about your conference experience.

The goals of family group conferencing are to provide a timely effective resolution to the incident, while providing the victim with direct input, and the offender the atmosphere to admit to the offense. The victims tell the offenders how the incident has affected their lives and the lives of their family. The victims and offenders then work together to repair the harm caused by the incident. This conference is provided as an alternative to court and provides timely consequences for the offender's behavior while bringing a sense of closure to both victim and offender.

The victim and offender are encouraged to include their supporters (close friends/family members). It is very important for both victim and offender to have supporters present. Victim supporters help victims express their feelings and desire, removing some of the anxiety and pressure victims may experience in a conference. Offender supporters help the offender deal with their behavior and begin to achieve re-integration. Everyone, whether victim, offender or supporter will be able to express their thoughts and feelings during the conference without interruption. Foul or abusive language will not be tolerated and may terminate the conference.

The conference process begins with full admissions from the offenders. Offender's motives are also discussed. The victims are then asked to talk about how the incident has affected their life. The supporters are then given an opportunity to speak. The conference then proceeds to repair the harm caused by the offender(s) actions. A contract created by the victim and offender is signed. If the conditions of the contract are not met, the incident can still be submitted for prosecution.

The conference process has been well received by the participants. This "Restorative Justice" has been used widely in Australia and New Zealand for many years, in America since 1994. The research results show a much lower level of future arrest by the offenders and higher level of satisfaction by the victim.

If you have any questions, please call the Woodbury Police Department at 739-4141.

RESTJUST/CONFLETTER

WE HELP
The Woodbury Way

152

Peer Conferencing Program

Case Flow Chart

Inform appropriate authority figures about case.

Speak with offender. Is offender willing to participate?

Does wrongdoer admit offense?

Tell what a conference is.

Tell the benefits the conference can do for him/her and for others.

Ask for participation.

Ask what happened in the incident.

Help wrongdoer to eliminate excuses, blaming and minimizing.

Who will their supporters be?

(Check for possible date, time, and supporters.)

Speak to Victim.

Tell who you are and why you are doing this.

Listen to their story. Listen! Listen! Listen!

Tell what a conference is.

Tell what good can come from it.

Ask for participation.

Ask what happened in the incident.

Tell what questions will be asked.

Who will their supporters be?

(Check for possible date, time, and supporters.)

Determine who else is appropriate to attend conference.

Speak to adults involved.

Set the meeting date, time, and place.

Check with everyone, be clear with directions.

Contact all participants.

Get refreshments and tissues.

Conduct conference.

Peer Conferencing Program

Conference Preparation

Victims

An important job we have as conference coordinators is to contact and listen to the victim—just listen. The conference facilitator needs to inform the victim about the process and the questions that will be presented to him/her. The victim will get to ask questions of the offender, tell the offender how their unacceptable behavior affected their lives, and ask the offender to repair the harm, as best as is possible.

"We want to offer you the opportunity to conference this incident in order to repair the harm that it has caused. _____ (name of offender) has agreed to participate. This will give you a chance to tell what happened, to ask questions, to tell how the incident affected you (how it hurt you/ how it made you feel). You will be able to tell _____ what you want for the future. You will have the opportunity to help to decide what the consequences will be for_____."

"I cannot promise that you will get what you want from the conference but people usually feel much better and are able to put the incident behind them."

"Will you come to the conference?"

"Who would you like to come with you? Who really cares about you?" *Don't take no for an answer here. It is essential that this person has someone there to be supportive and to speak.*

Get names and the phone numbers of supporters to be called, if necessary.

Peer Conferencing Program

Conference Preparation

Offender

When contacting the offender cover these four parts:

1. We need to ask the offender to participate. "The incident that happened the other day caused some harm and having a conference could repair the harm and resolve the problem. It would be a good thing to do for you and it would be good for (*the victim*). You could bring some supporters with you. Would you be willing to come?"

2. The person who has done the harm must admit that he/she has done something wrong and be willing to say so WITH NO EXCUSES. If there are any complicating circumstances (and there often are) the offender must wait until later in the conference to bring them up. (Usually other people bring up the complications and the person does not need to defend him/herself.) The initial statements in the conference ought to be a clear admission that the person did the act and is fully owning it.

"If you had it to do over again would you do it differently? Why?"
"Can you tell others in the conference what you did wrong?"
Listen to them tell the story. *Is it OK or are there excuses being made?* Stay with the offender until they can tell the story of the incident without minimizing it and without any excuses or blaming others.

3. Prepare the offender for the questions he/she will hear during the conference. "I will ask you to tell the story of what happened, and who was affected by the incident. Do you think you can answer those questions?"

4. Ask who should be invited to participate in the conference. "Who cares about you? Who would you like to support you in the conference?" This may be harder than with the victim but it is VERY important that people who are special to the wrongdoer be there to support him/her, even if the offender does not want them there. *Don't take no for an answer here. It is essential that this person has someone there besides the parents to be supportive.*

The benefits to the offender are that he/she can right the wrong, leave behind the offender label, be seen as a good person who made a mistake.

Peer Conferencing Program

Conference Preparation
Supporters

Your job here usually is fairly easy. By the time you are speaking to supporters, the place, date, and time of the conference is usually set up. The supporter is either clearly associated with the incident or has been nominated. An invitation and explanation usually will be all that is needed.

"We are having a conference about the incident that happened which involved so-and-so and so-and-so. _____ asked if you could be there as a supporter. We want you to just sit near him/her and answer some questions about what you thought or felt about the incident. Then we will all try to repair the harm done by the inappropriate behavior and come to some agreement. Do you think you would be able to come?"

Be ready to answer any questions.

Peer Conferencing Program

An observer may sit outside the circle and can collect feedback for the facilitator through observation.

Be the guardian of the process and interrupt people if necessary to refocus the conference or to maintain a safe environment.

Do not contribute to the conference yourself. You are privileged to assist these people in solving their own problem. You do not by rights belong there but are being allowed.

All participation and agreements are voluntary.

If necessary:

• Stop a put-down.

• Stop any name calling.

• Remind participants that we are here to repair the harm.

• Remind people that we are NOT here to decide if this person is a good or bad person.

Appendix III
Facilitator Training Notes
and Training Agenda

REAL JUSTICE INTRODUCTION VIDEO
Introduction to Conferencing

REAL JUSTICE is based on the scripted model of conferencing implemented by police in Wagga Wagga, New South Wales, Australia in 1991.

To be eligible for a conference offenders must admit to the offense.

After the offenders tell what they did, victims and others tell how they were affected.

After everyone has spoken, the group decides how to repair the harm which almost always results in a written agreement.

Refreshments, a symbolic "breaking of bread," are always served after the conference, which allows for further reintegration, healing and closure.

Conferencing originated in New Zealand, where it is called "family group conferencing." It was established by a 1989 law based on indigenous Maori tradition.

The first school conference was run by a guidance counselor in Maroochydore High School, Queensland in 1994.

REAL JUSTICE meets the needs of victims more than courts or school disciplinary procedures.

REAL JUSTICE teaches empathy so that offenders begin to connect their wrongdoing. to other people's feelings.

REAL JUSTICE changes the role of police in the eyes of offenders and the community.

Conferences can be used in a variety of settings with offenders of all ages.

Conferences can be held after serious offenses go to court.

REAL JUSTICE changes the way that schools handle discipline, creating a healthier school environment.

REAL JUSTICE FACILITATION VIDEO
How to Facilitate a Conference

Begin by seating participants according to a prearranged seating chart.

PREAMBLE
The facilitator now sets the focus for the conference.

INTRODUCTION
Note that the facilitator never uses the word "offender."

Note that the offender is told that this is voluntary and that the conference may be terminated at any time but, that then the matter will be referred to formal proceedings.

THE OFFENDER'S STORY
At this point the facilitator asks the offender to talk about what happened and how people have been affected.

THE VICTIM'S STORY
The facilitator then asks the victims to explain how they have been affected. Note that the facilitator does not nod or affirm but, merely thanks each participant when they are finished speaking.

VICTIM SUPPORTERS
At this point the facilitator asks the victim supporters to talk about how they were affected.

OFFENDER SUPPORTERS
Now the facilitator asks the offender's supporters to discuss how they have been affected.
Note that the facilitator does not respond to questions, but redirects to the individual or to the group.

THE AGREEMENT PHASE
Note that the facilitator refrains from making suggestions, limiting his responses to clarification.

In the Agreement Phase the victims are first asked what they want to see come out of today's conference.
Note that the facilitator continues to ask questions to assist the group in specifying the details of the agreement. The facilitator checks each item of the agreement with the participants involved.

When the facilitator senses that people are finished, he begins to bring the conference to a close, but is open to suggestions or comments.

REINTEGRATION
The facilitator prepares the contract, allowing participants to interact informally while having refreshments.

<u>REAL</u> JUSTICE FACILITATION VIDEO
Why Does <u>REAL</u> JUSTICE WORK?

***Changing Lenses*, by Howard Zehr**

<u>REAL</u> JUSTICE works by meeting the emotional needs of victims.

    Need opportunity to express their feelings

    Need to hear acknowledgment from loved ones

    Need assurance that what happened was unfair and undeserved

    Need direct contact with offenders

    If possible, hear the offender:

        • express shame and remorse

        • answer questions about crime

        • assure it won't happen again

    Need a sense of safety

Participation in the <u>conference must be the victim's choice</u>.

<u>REAL</u> JUSTICE works on an emotional basis to meet these needs of victims.

***Crime, Shame and Reintegration*, by John Braithwaite**

(pages 25-26 in manual)

The free expression of emotion also impacts offenders.

Offenders experience shame in two ways:

    • Externally, through sanctions or condemnation by family, friends or community

    • Internally, through a socialized sense of right and wrong — a conscience.

Reintegrative shaming occurs in the context of care and support.

Reintegrative shaming distinguishes between the deed and the doer:

        • Unacceptable behavior is rejected.

        • Individual's worth is affirmed.

Our current systems fail to make the distinction between the deed and the doer.

Our criminal justice and school disciplinary procedures stigmatize because they usually fail to offer the wrongdoer an opportunity to shed the offender label.

Stigmatization fosters negative subcultures.

Societies that reintegrate offenders rather than stigmatize have less crime.

Courts exclude those most affected by the crime.

Schools also exclude victims and others.

CURRENT SYSTEMS (Retributive Justice)	REAL JUSTICE (Restorative Justice)
Offense defined as violation against the system	Offense defined as harm to persons or the community
Focus on establishing blame, on guilt, on past behavior	Focus on problem-solving, on repairing the harm
Victim ignored	Victim rights and needs recognized
Offender passive	Offender encouraged to take responsibility
Offender accountability defined as punishment	Offender accountability defined as demonstrating empathy and helping to repair the harm
Response focused on offender's past behavior	Response focused on harmful consequences of offender's behavior
Stigma of crime unremovable	Stigma of crime removable through appropriate actions
Little encouragement for repentance and forgiveness	Repentance is encouraged and forgiveness is possible
Dependence upon professionals	Direct involvement of those affected by the incident
Strictly rational process	Allows for free expression of emotion

(Adapted from Howard Zehr)

Shame and Pride, **by Donald Nathanson** (pages 23-25 in manual)
Affect Theory of Silvan S. Tomkins

Affects/emotion are fundamentally in all of us, developed for adaptive responses for survival.
There are nine basic affects/emotions.
In a conference we are moving from the most toxic or negative emotions to the more positive emotions.
Dissmell, the most toxic of the emotions, protects us from poisoning.
Contempt is dissmell combined with anger.

NEGATIVE AFFECTS
    Dissmell
    Anger - Rage
    Fear - Terror
    Disgust
    Distress - Anguish
    Shame

The emotion of shame indicates a wish to restore bonds with others.
Tomkins described shame as "one step away from Heaven."
Shame occurs when there is a barrier to joy or interest.

NEUTRAL
    Surprise - Startle

POSITIVE
    Interest - Excitement
    Enjoyment - Joy

Affective resonance fosters shared feelings.
REAL JUSTICE conferencing builds community.
REAL JUSTICE works through the free expression of emotion.
It minimizes the negative emotions and maximizes the positive.

REAL JUSTICE FACILITATION VIDEO
Before the Conference

The offender must admit to the offense to be eligible for a conference.

Before the conference, if possible, the facilitator should encourage the offender to take full responsibility.

Sometimes a personal visit may be necessary to accomplish that or to get the offender and family to participate at all.

The facilitator should work with the offender until he takes responsibility and stops blaming others.

When the offender takes adequate responsibility, the facilitator may move on.

To save the victim any disappointment, the facilitator first makes sure the offender has agreed to come.

A personal visit with the victim is preferable, although not always feasible.

The victim's preference for a meeting time should be given the greatest weight.

The facilitator now contacts the victim and offender supporters. Their comments may offer a wider perspective on the incident.

But the facilitator should not offer opinions, except to express empathy or disapproval of the inappropriate act.

The facilitator checks that everyone knows how to get to the conference location and has transportation.

The facilitator ensures that the conference will be held without interruptions in a comfortable location.

The facilitator carefully plans for all the details, from seating and refreshments to the box of tissues, which incidentally lets participants know that displays of emotion are okay.

TWO-DAY TRAINING AGENDA

Day One:	**Orientation**
7:45-8:00	Registration and Coffee
8:00-8:30	Introductions and Expectations
8:30-8:50	"Introduction to Conferencing" Video
8:50-9:15	System Goals and Achievements
9:15-9:45	Doing the Right Thing
9:45-10:15	Victim Needs
10:15-10:30	Break
10:30-10:35	Varied Uses of Conferencing
10:35-11:25	"How to Facilitate a Conference" Video
11:25-11:40	Gathering Questions
11:40-12:00	"Why Does REAL JUSTICE Work?" Video
12:00-1:00	Lunch
1:00-1:30	Questions and Answers
1:30-2:30	1st Mini Role Play
2:30-2:45	Break
2:45-3:05	Appropriate Conferences
3:05-3:25	"Something Different" Video
3:25-3:40	More Questions and Answers
3:40-3:45	REAL JUSTICE Services
3:45-4:00	Wrap-up

Before Day Two, participants may wish to look through the manual and especially review the Conference Facilitator Script.

Day Two:	**Facilitating Conferences**
7:45-8:00	Sign-in and Coffee
8:00-8:05	Response to Feedback
8:05-8:30	"Before the Conference" Video
8:30-9:30	2nd Mini Role Play
9:30-10:30	3rd Mini Role Play
10:30-10:45	Break
10:45-11:45	4th Mini Role Play
11:45-12:00	More Questions and Answers
12:00-1:00	Lunch
1:00-2:30	Large Role Play
2:30-2:45	Break
2:45-3:45	Implementation Planning
3:45-4:00	Wrap-up

Some trainings may vary from this two-day schedule, but the sequence and time allotted for each training activity will stay the same.